P9-BYQ-880

3 2224 00232 4778

Student Handbook to Psychology

History, Perspectives, and Applications

Volume I

Student Handbook to Psychology

History, Perspectives, and Applications

Volume I

KENNETH D. KEITH

Bernard C. Beins
General Editor

Facts On File
An Infobase Learning Company

For Dave, Kelly, Heather, and Steve

Student Handbook to Psychology: History, Perspectives, and Applications
Copyright © 2012 Kenneth D. Keith

Facts On File, Inc.
An Imprint of Infobase Learning
132 West 31st Street
New York NY 10001

Library of Congress Cataloging-in-Publication Data
Student handbook to psychology / [edited by] Bernard C. Beins.
  v. ; cm.
  Includes bibliographical references and index.
  Contents: v. 1. History, perspectives, and applications / Kenneth D. Keith—v. 2. Methods and measurements / Bernard C. Beins—v. 3. Brain and mind / Michael Kerchner—v. 4. Learning and thinking / Christopher M. Hakala and Bernard C. Beins—v. 5. Developmental psychology / Lynn Shelley—v. 6. Personality and abnormal psychology / Janet F. Carlson—v. 7. Social psychology / Jeffrey D. Holmes and Sheila K. Singh.
  ISBN 978-0-8160-8280-3 (set : alk. paper)—ISBN 978-0-8160-8281-0 (v. 1 : alk. paper)—ISBN 978-0-8160-8286-5 (v. 2 : alk. paper)—ISBN 978-0-8160-8285-8 (v. 3 : alk. paper)—ISBN 978-0-8160-8284-1 (v. 4 : alk. paper)—ISBN 978-0-8160-8282-7 (v. 5 : alk. paper)—ISBN 978-0-8160-8287-2 (v. 6 : alk. paper)—ISBN 978-0-8160-8283-4 (v. 7 : alk. paper) 1. Psychology—Textbooks. I. Beins, Bernard.
  BF121.S884 2012
  150—dc23   2011045277

Text design by Erika K. Arroyo
Cover design by Takeshi Takahashi
Composition by EJB Publishing Services
Cover printed by Yurchak Printing, Landisville, Pa.
Book printed and bound by Yurchak Printing, Landisville, Pa.
Date printed: September 2012
Printed in the United States of America

This book is printed on acid-free paper.

CONTENTS

PREFACE

Behavior is endlessly fascinating. People and other animals are complicated creatures that show extraordinary patterns of abilities, intelligence, social interaction, and creativity along with, unfortunately, problematic behaviors. All of these characteristics emerge because of the way the brain interprets incoming information and directs our responses to that information.

This seven-volume **Student Handbook to Psychology** set highlights important and interesting facets of thought and behavior. It provides a solid foundation for learning about psychological processes associated with growth and development, social issues, thinking and problem solving, and abnormal thought and behavior. Most of the major schools and theories related to psychology appear in the books in the series, albeit in abbreviated form. Because psychology is such a highly complex and diverse discipline, these volumes present a broad overview of the subject rather than a complete and definitive treatise. Such a work, in fact, would be difficult (if not impossible) because psychological scientists are still searching for answers to a great number of questions. If you are interested in delving in more depth into specific areas of psychology, we have provided a bibliography of accessible readings to help you fill in the details.

The volumes in this series follow the order that you might see in a standard presentation on a variety of topics, but each book stands alone and the series does not need to be read in any particular order. In fact, you can peruse individual chapters in each volume at will, seeking out and focusing on those topics that interest you most. On the other hand, if you do choose to read through a complete volume, you will find a flow of information that connects related sections of the books, providing a coherent overview of the entire discipline of psychology.

The authors of the seven volumes in this series are experts in their respective fields, so you will find psychological concepts that are up to date and that reflect the most recent advances in scientific knowledge about thought and behavior. In addition, each of the authors is an excellent writer who has presented the information in an interesting and compelling fashion. Although some of the material and many of the ideas are complex, the authors have done an outstanding job of conveying those ideas in ways that are both interesting and effective.

In *History, Perspectives, and Applications*, Professor Kenneth Keith of the University of San Diego has woven historical details into a tapestry that shows how psychological questions originated within a philosophical framework, incorporated biological concepts, and ultimately evolved into a single scientific discipline that remains interconnected with many other academic and scientific disciplines. Dr. Keith has identified the major figures associated with the development of the field of psychology as well as the social forces that helped shape their ideas.

In *Methods and Measurements*, I illustrate how psychologists create new knowledge through research. The volume presents the major approaches to research and explains how psychologists develop approaches to research that help us answer questions about complex aspects of behavior. Without these well-structured and proven research methods, we would not have much of the information we now have about behavior. Furthermore, these methods, approaches, and practices provide confidence that the knowledge we do have is good knowledge, grounded in solid research.

Many people are under the impression that each thought or behavior is a single thing. In *Brain and Mind*, Professor Michael Kerchner of Washington College dispels this impression by showing how the myriad structures and functions of our brain work in unison to create those seemingly simple and one-dimensional behaviors. As the author explains, each behavior is really the result of many different parts of the brain engaging in effective communication with one another. Professor Kerchner also explains what occurs when this integration breaks down.

Learning and Thinking, co-authored by Professor Christopher Hakala of Western New England College and me (at Ithaca College), explores the fascinating field of cognitive psychology, a discipline focused on the processes by which people learn, solve problems, and display intelligence. Cognitive psychology is a fascinating field that explores how we absorb information, integrate it, and then act on it.

In *Developmental Psychology*, Professor Lynn Shelley of Westfield State University addresses the very broad area of psychology that examines how people develop and change from the moment of conception through old age. Dr. Shelley's detailed and compelling explanation includes a focus on how maturation and environment play a part in shaping how each individual grows, evolves, and changes.

In *Personality and Abnormal Psychology*, Professor Janet Carlson of the Buros Center for Testing at the University of Nebraska (Lincoln) addresses various dimensions of personality, highlighting processes that influence normal and abnormal facets of personality. Dr. Carlson also explains how psychologists study the fundamental nature of personality and how it unfolds.

The final volume in this series is *Social Psychology*. Co-authored by Professor Jeffrey Holmes of Ithaca College and Sheila Singh of Cornell University, this volume examines how our thoughts and behaviors emerge in connection with our interactions with other people. As the authors of this volume explain, changes in a person's social environment can lead to notable changes in the way that person thinks and behaves.

As editor of this series, I have had the opportunity to work with all of the authors who have contributed their expertise and insights to this project. During this collaborative process, I found that we have much in common. All of us have spent our careers pondering why people think and act the way they do. For every answer we come up with, we also develop new questions that are just as interesting and important. And we all agree that you cannot find a more interesting subject to study than psychology.

As you learn about psychology, we hope that the information in these seven volumes inspires the same fascination in you. We also hope that our explanations, illustrations, and narrative studies motivate you to continue studying why we humans are the way we are.

—Bernard C. Beins, Ph.D., Professor of Psychology,
Ithaca College, Series Editor

INTRODUCTION

The public perception of psychology has long been fraught with confusion and misunderstanding. Many people seem unaware of the distinction between psychology and the medical specialty of psychiatry, and students who come to the field often expect to find a field exclusively devoted to the care and treatment of individuals with personal problems. Unfortunately, many members of the public never have the opportunity to learn more—about the origins of psychology, about its scientific foundations, or about recent developments that strengthen the ability of psychologists to apply their science to improvement of the human condition.

Broadly speaking, psychology has two major aims. *First,* researchers are actively engaged in scientific investigations intended to create and disseminate new knowledge in a broad range of subjects related to the behavior both of humans and of nonhuman animals. Much of this research takes place in university settings, sometimes in collaboration not only among psychologists, but also with those who work in other disciplines, such as biology, medicine, or education. *Second,* psychologists aim to improve the lives of people through application of knowledge in a variety of venues and through various means. Some of these are obvious, for example, diagnosis and treatment of mental illness or counseling in vocational or educational settings. But psychologists also work in a surprisingly broad array of applied areas, ranging from law to medicine to social policy, and more.

This book serves as an introduction to the field of psychology, from its historical origins in the scientific and human concerns of people who did not yet have the term *psychology* available to label their interests, to the basic research of scientists using the latest electronic technology to improve the lives of people with seriously debilitating illnesses. Along the way you will get a glimpse of the life and times of some of psychology's celebrities, and we will meet some of the field's greatest contributors whose names remain unknown to most people outside the field. Human behavior has an obvious inherent interest for us all; after all, as psychologist B.F. Skinner once noted, we are always in the presence of at least one behaving organism—ourselves. For this reason as well as many others, I hope this volume will inspire you to broaden your interest and deepen your knowledge about psychology.

Kenneth D. Keith, San Diego

CHAPTER 1

PSYCHOLOGY: A LONG PAST AND A SHORT HISTORY

Twenty-first century **psychology** is the science of behavior and mental processes, and ranks as one of the most popular majors in American colleges and universities. Modern psychological scientists are on the cutting edge of research in many fields: neuroscience, behavioral medicine, human perception, cross-cultural understanding, and many others. These contemporary interests might lead you to logically conclude that psychology is a new, up and coming area of study—and you would be right, to the extent that psychologists are always developing new information and extending the limits of human knowledge. But it may surprise you to learn that psychology is also one of the oldest areas of scholarly interest. Yet for much of this very long past, the field we know as psychology was initially of interest to philosophers and then to scientists trained in biology and physiology. It is only in the last 150 years or so that psychology has come into its own as a distinct discipline. It was this contradiction that prompted the German psychologist Hermann Ebbinghaus, writing in 1908, to say that "Psychology has a long past, yet its real history is short." In this chapter, we will briefly review the history of psychology, from the days of classical Greece to the psychological perspectives that have characterized the field in the past century.

THE ANCIENTS
As early as the 7th century B.C.E., Egyptian Pharaoh Psamtik I conducted research that we might consider psychological in nature. Psamtik believed

Egyptians to be the world's most ancient people, and he set out to design an experiment to prove it. Assuming that people had an inborn ability to use language, Psamtik reasoned that a child isolated from birth, and hearing no spoken language, would eventually speak its inborn language. That first language, Psamtik believed, would have to be the natural first language of humans; he further assumed the language would be Egyptian.

Cruel as it may seem, Psamtik took two babies from their mother and arranged for them to live in an isolated area where they would receive physical care but hear no spoken language. Fortunately, the children did learn to speak, but their language refuted Psamtik's hypothesis; the children's first words were not Egyptian, but the language of Phrygia—an ancient country located in what is now modern-day Turkey! Although his research was crudely designed, psychologists studying language today would recognize Psamtik's early interest as a classic problem in nature/nurture, or **genetics**/environment.

Two or three centuries later, such Greek philosophers and physicians as Socrates (469–399 B.C.E.), Hippocrates (the father of medicine, who lived 460–377 B.C.E.), Plato (429–347 B.C.E.), and Aristotle (384–322 B.C.E.) struggled to understand many of the issues that continue to attract the interest of today's psychologists—issues like memory, learning, dreaming, functions and disorders of the **brain**, and our perception of the world around us. Aristotle's *History of Animals* stood for 20 centuries as the greatest existing work on biology. But it is likely that he was also the first person to attempt a true discussion of psychology, which resulted in a work titled *De Anima* ("On the Mind"). It is small wonder then that the word *psychology* comes from the Greek *psyche*, meaning the soul or the mind. The Greeks attempted to free scientific explanation from religious, supernatural forces, and made efforts to account for empirical (observed) events in the world around them. Hippocrates, for example, thought of the brain as the seat of **consciousness** and intellect, and he believed that problems of thinking and behavior were the result of pathology in the brain, rather than punishment from the gods (as many people of the time believed). At the same time, however, the Greeks did not usually conduct experiments in the sense that today's psychologists might—by manipulating variables and collecting data to test specific hypotheses. Although the Greek scholars were interested in the same kinds of questions about human nature as interest contemporary psychologists, their approach was more often philosophical, involving general theories and speculations. Nevertheless, the ancient Greeks left us with scientific ideas that, in some ways, laid the groundwork for modern psychology; for example, Aristotle's notions of mental states predated somewhat similar ideas in the 20th-century field of cognitive psychology, and Socrates taught his pupils using a questioning approach that in the 21st century we might call the discovery method of teaching.

Bust of Aristotle *(Wikipedia)*

Later, in Rome, the great physician Galen (130–200 C.E.) brought together his knowledge of the wisdom of the Greeks, his dissections of nonhuman animals, and his observations and experience as a doctor. He eventually concluded that the problems he called "diseases of the soul" came from human emotions like fear, anger, lust, envy, and grief; he claimed that we must work for self-understanding—a goal that is difficult to achieve because we are blind to our own faults and therefore requires the assistance of a mature outsider. Galen's assessment may well have a familiar ring if you have given any thought to the relationship existing between psychotherapists and their clients.

The Roman Age during which Galen lived produced significant technological advances in engineering, mechanics, and transportation. The Romans were great builders, developing roads to move people, aqueducts to move water, and baths for health and relaxation. Examples of all these technical achievements remain today in far-flung locations that were part of the Roman Empire (For instance, in the city of Bath, in England, visitors can taste water from springs feeding the great Roman baths that are preserved there). However, despite their technological abilities, and their respect for the accomplishments of the Greeks, the Romans did not produce great science, and science in fact declined along with the Roman Empire. Galen, and his science, therefore stood out among the

Roman Baths in England *(David Iliff. Wikipedia)*

Romans, and even after the decline of the Roman Empire (which historians place in the late 5th century C.E.) his views dominated medicine for many years to come, throughout the Middle (Medieval) Ages (from about the 5th century C.E. and lasting for 1,000 years or so).

MOVING FORWARD: BACKDROP TO A SCIENCE
The Middle Ages
Although many writers referred to the Middle Ages as the Dark Ages because of the decline in European civilization, the era was not without its advances in technology, scholarship, and science. For example, the Middle Ages gave rise to the windmill, the printing press, gunpowder, gear for effective use of horses (bits, bridles, stirrups), the clock, gothic architecture, and numerous great European universities (e.g., Oxford, Cambridge, Paris, and Bologna). Windmills and watermills, both developed in Asia, were widespread in Europe by the year 1000, with nearly 6,000 watermills in Britain alone by the 11th century. However, the questions we might call psychological were largely the province of religion during the Middle Ages, and years of conflict and upheaval intervened before the universities became centers of real scientific development.

In the meantime, despite some progressive ideas from Arab scholars, science was based on untested assumptions—untested not only due to the absence of scientific methods, but also because there was little interest in challenging religious views of nature. It was during this time that St. Thomas Aquinas (1225–1274) tried to reconcile the differences between reason and religious faith, presenting an argument for the dualism dividing body and soul (or mind)—a distinction that psychologists still debate today. The population of Europe declined significantly in the Middle Ages, mostly because of successive waves of epidemic disease. The best known of these was the bubonic plague, which resulted in the "Black Death" of 1348–1350. Approximately one-quarter of the European population died in these epidemics, perhaps 40 million or more people.

The Renaissance
In the 1300s, change gradually came to Europe. In the university city of Bologna, for example, students were introduced to the study of human anatomy and women were permitted to become professors. The poet Petrarch became known throughout Europe, and art and literature began to flourish in Italy. By the year 1500, a time commonly assigned to the emergence of the European Renaissance, there were signs of a new age in the history of the world. The Renaissance was particularly linked to developments in art, and in the 15th and 16th centuries, the printed book allowed wider audiences access to such important works as Chaucer's *Canterbury Tales* as well as to other works of literature, history, philosophy, and technology. Although the Chinese had produced printed

Balliol College, Oxford University *(Toby Ord. Wikipedia)*

manuscripts several centuries earlier, it was Johannes Gutenberg's invention of movable type around 1450 that made book printing cheap and efficient. The widespread availability of printed material changed the Renaissance world as much as television changed the world of the 20th century or the Internet changed the 21st.

But despite scholarly advances, including those associated with the scientific genius of Leonardo da Vinci (1452–1519), science moved forward at a slow pace. The culture did not demand scientific ideas, and there were no microscopes, telescopes, or major laboratories. The religious notion of the unique and special creation of humankind made biological study of the origins of humans seem unnecessary and even dangerous. Before long, however, an Englishman named Francis Bacon (1561–1626) would predict a new age of learning that, he expected, would surpass the Greeks and the Romans. Writing at the beginning of the 1600s, Bacon advocated a new science, dedicated to the idea that humans could reveal and understand the secrets of nature through observation and experimentation. He believed science should be dedicated to enriching human life. Following on the heels of Bacon, another Englishman,

Isaac Newton (1642–1727), produced major advances in science, not only in his monumental work on the nature of gravity (reported in *Principia Mathematica*), but also in his refraction of light into its elements—a model that would guide the later efforts of the British empiricist philosophers in their effort to understand the elements of consciousness.

At more or less the same time as Bacon was promoting observation and experimentation with nature, French philosopher and mathematician René Descartes (1596–1650) was developing a new conceptual model of human functioning. Descartes proposed a **dualistic** (two-part) mind-body model, with the body a machine-like, reflexive physical system and the mind an immaterial (non-physical) seat of thought and consciousness. The mind, Descartes believed, could control certain of the body's reflexes, and the body-machine's movements were enabled by the movement of fluids in hollow tubes throughout the body. The entire mind-body interaction, according to Descartes, was choreographed via the pineal gland, a tiny structure in the brain.

Although Descartes (as we now know) had many of the facts wrong, he laid the groundwork for the study of reflexes and for the central role of the brain. But because his views questioned traditional religious principles by seeking earth-bound explanations for physical phenomena, they posed a serious challenge to the church, which placed his works on the *Index of Prohibited Books*. Nonetheless, further efforts to deal with the problem of mind-body dualism have continued to characterize much of psychology since the time of Descartes. Another problem for Descartes, one that also troubled philosophers who followed him, was the issue of how humans recognize reality and distinguish it from the images created by our thoughts and ideas about reality. This problem was compounded by Descartes' belief that some ideas were innate (inborn) and not a product of experience with the environment. These, he thought, included ideas about time and space, God, self, and geometry.

Empiricism

English philosopher Thomas Hobbes (1588–1679) became a friend of Descartes but did not accept his notion of innate ideas. Instead Hobbes believed that ideas come from sensory experience, making him, in the eyes of some historians, a psychological empiricist. His views anticipated those of the British empiricists who followed him, of whom John Locke (1632–1704) was one of the most prominent. Locke's *An Essay Concerning Human Understanding*, written in 1690, marked a significant beginning for British empiricism. In arguing for the singular role of experience as the source of ideas, he famously characterized the mind as a blank page upon which experience writes—an idea, by the way, that did not originate with Locke. Centuries before, Aristotle had similarly described the mind as a blank tablet.

For Locke, experience gained via the senses and subsequent reflection upon that experience constituted the sources of all ideas. Because we remember sensory experience, Locke believed, we can therefore reflect on objects not present, giving us the ability to generate ideas independent of immediate sensations. Locke's position on the importance of experience gained support from a very interesting line of research. One of Locke's friends wondered whether a person blind from birth, who knew common objects only by touch, would recognize them if he or she were later able to see. Locke reasoned that the person would need to have some visual experience with the objects before developing the ability to visually identify them. During the 18th century, the development of surgery to remove congenital cataracts allowed study of precisely such patients; and, as Locke predicted, they required visual experience before they could recognize common objects.

Locke's belief in the power of environment to provide formative experience was clear not only in his published writings, but also in letters he wrote to a

John Locke on Parenting

Although he did not have children, John Locke, in the late 17th century, was happy to write letters filled with childrearing advice to his cousin Mary Clarke and her husband Edward. He made recommendations related to various aspects of behavioral and educational development of their children, and he also had ideas about the different approaches parents should use for rearing boys and girls. He wrote that children should be encouraged in cultivating sound minds as well as sound bodies. His advice included such body-toughening ideas as washing children's feet in cold water and providing them with leaky shoes, so they would become able to avoid the ills associated with cold, wet feet. In a foreshadowing of the techniques behaviorists would develop three centuries later, he advocated introducing the cold water gradually, beginning with lukewarm water and then making it colder and colder day by day.

Locke also had ideas about developing the intellect of children. They should start, he said, with reading material that was easy and pleasant—he recommended *Aesop's Fables*, for example. He valued reason and virtue above all else, and considered dancing important for the grace, manliness, and confidence it could instill. On the other hand, he considered music a wasteful enterprise, not only because it would take a great deal of time to learn, but also because it would bring children in contact with "odd company." In his view, only poetry was less desirable than music!

Source: Benjamin, L.T., Jr. 2006. *A History of Psychology in Letters*, 2nd ed. Malden, Mass.: Blackwell Publishing.

cousin, giving a variety of kinds of childrearing advice. Locke is important to the history of psychology for at least two key reasons. First, his work (as well as the work of the empiricists who followed him) served to break down prior psychological ideas based on intuitive and supernatural assumptions about the mind and soul. Second, the empiricists set the stage for the data-based **experimental psychology** that was to follow.

Associationism

Scottish-born David Hume (1711–1776) wanted to develop what he called a "science of man," by which he essentially meant psychology. One of his best-known works is *An Enquiry Concerning Human Understanding.* Published in 1748, this work promoted the idea of the new science of human nature, distinct from philosophy. Hume followed in the footsteps of the earlier empiricists but went beyond them in his effort to account for the *associations* between sensory impressions and ideas. Ideas become associated, he argued, for one of three reasons: resemblance (similarity), **contiguity** (proximity in time and place), or cause and effect. With regard to the last of these, cause and effect, Hume believed that we cannot experience causality directly; we can only observe that one event reliably follows, or occurs along with, another. Although we may infer that one causes the other, their association (correlation) alone does not *prove* a causal relation. It is an idea espoused by psychological scientists to this day.

Hume's contemporary, David Hartley (1705–1757), applied the idea of association to the brain, basing his view on the notion that such phenomena as ideas and vibrations, if they occur together enough times, will become associated. In connection with this, he argued that if a vibration later occurs, it will cause the mind (brain) to produce a "miniature" (or image) of the associated stimulus. Hartley was a careful observer and accurately described such psychophysiological processes as afterimages (i.e., after viewing a light, we may continue to see a brief image of the light after it is extinguished; or we may experience a parallel auditory process—briefly hearing a musical note or chord even after the original sound stimulus is gone). Associations, Hartley thought, could be extended to motor behaviors in explaining learning and the formation of habits; thus, the association of simpler motor behaviors would allow people to master such complex skills as piano playing. He believed in the continuity between human and animal psychology, and although it would be more than a century before the field of physiological psychology would come into existence, Hartley's observations prepared the way for it. His ideas also influenced the thinking of a prominent British father and son team of associationists, James Mill (1773–1836) and John Stuart Mill (1806–1873).

James Mill used the metaphor of a house to illustrate his view of association. Both brick and mortar, he pointed out, are complex ideas; combining these ideas with the additional ideas of position and quantity can make a wall. He applied his belief in the power of experience to the personal tutoring of his son, John Stuart Mill, providing his offspring exposure to advanced educational opportunities from an early age. The younger Mill began learning Greek at age 3 and Latin a few years later. By the age of 10, he had read many Greek and Roman classics; by the age of 11, he was writing about Roman government. Although John Stuart Mill had acquired the equivalent of a university education by the age of 12, he always insisted that his intellect was no greater than that of other children and that his accomplishments were merely a reflection of the efforts and methods his father had used to teach him.

John Stuart Mill built upon the empiricist and associationist ideas of his father and of those (such as Hartley) who had come before. He used the model of chemical (rather than mechanical) associations to explain development of complex ideas. He further expanded his father's metaphor, observing that when mortar and brick combined to make a wall, the resulting structure actually had new characteristics that differed from those of its elements, essentially creating a whole that was greater than the sum of its parts. In 1843, Mill set forth his mental chemistry and views of association, presenting the case for the scientific study of psychology, which he defined as "the science of the elementary laws of the mind." Psychology (like other sciences), Mill believed, should rely on experimental methods, meaning it must move from speculation to a science based on observation and experiment. However, recognizing the ethical limits of experimentation on some important human institutions (e.g., social class, education, family characteristics), Mill worked at developing logical means to determine causality from observations of naturally occurring human events—an approach not unlike the longitudinal methods used by modern-day **developmental psychologists** as they follow children over time.

Despite the reservations of other European philosophers, like Gottfried Wilhelm Leibniz (1646–1716) and Immanuel Kant (1724–1804), psychology was well on its way to becoming a science. The 19th century would be a crucial proving ground as the influences of philosophy, **physiology**, and physics converged in the move toward a distinct new discipline—but not until a prescientific, public-oriented phase had run its course.

Prescientific "Healers"

The possibility of self-improvement and healing has long been appealing to people with problems. This was as true in the 18th and 19th centuries as it is in the 21st, and at least two such approaches found widespread appeal among audiences on both sides of the Atlantic Ocean. Both of these were eventually recognized as pseudoscience (views or theories mistakenly assumed to be scientific), but not before achieving great popularity.

Mesmerism

You have probably heard the term *mesmerism*, which generally means a kind of animal magnetism or hypnotic appeal. The word comes from the name of Franz Anton Mesmer (1734–1815), an Austrian doctor who believed that his patients' problems, especially those with possible psychological causes, were the result of magnetic disharmonies or imbalances in their bodies. He claimed to be able to cure these disorders by passing magnets over patients' bodies, in the process putting these people into a trance; when they came out of the trance, according to Mesmer, their health would be restored.

Mesmer first worked his magic in Vienna, where the medical community was very critical, eventually ordering him to cease practicing medicine there. Mesmer then moved to Paris, where he was a colorful, flamboyant performer who attracted patients from the wealthy members of Parisian society. When French doctors also questioned the validity of mesmerism and labeled Mesmer a fraud, King Louis XVI appointed a scientific commission (headed by American Benjamin Franklin) to investigate. This group, like the Viennese doctors, found that Mesmer's treatment had no basis in science. This did not stop Mesmer, who continued his practice before eventually retiring to a secluded life in Switzerland. Mesmer had many followers, not only in France but also in England, and these adherents of mesmerism carried the practice to the United States, where it remained popular with some people until the beginning of the 20th century. Eventually, mesmerists moved away from the use of magnets, focusing more on trances. In the mid-19th century trances led to hypnosis, which (in 1882) the French Academy of Sciences recognized as a legitimate process.

Phrenology and Physiognomy

A few years after the Austrian Mesmer gained fame for his magnet treatments, a German named Franz Josef Gall (1758–1828) built a strong reputation for his work in advancing understanding of the anatomy of the brain and the function of **nerve** fibers. One of Gall's especially important contributions was demonstrating the fact that each half of the brain controls the opposite side of the body (what we today call **contralateral function**). He also receives credit for the idea of localization of the functions of the brain—the notion that specific areas of the brain control specific human actions and characteristics. Although the particular features of his view of localization proved to be incorrect, Gall's ideas of localization, as well as the associated view that the shape of the head also related to specific characteristics, led to a second pseudoscientific perspective: **phrenology**.

The term phrenology ("study of the mind"), which Gall also called "cranioscopy," referred to the belief that the shape of the head, and the bumps and indentations of the skull, were indicators of various aspects of an individual's

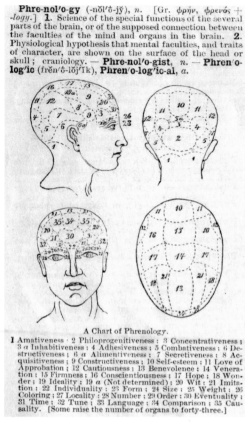

Phre-nol'o-gy (-nŏl'ō-jȳ), *n.* [Gr. φρήν, φρενός + *-logy.*] **1.** Science of the special functions of the several parts of the brain, or of the supposed connection between the faculties of the mind and organs in the brain. **2.** Physiological hypothesis that mental faculties, and traits of character, are shown on the surface of the head or skull; craniology. — **Phre-nol'o-gist,** *n.* — **Phren'o-log'ic** (frĕn'ō-lŏj'ĭk), **Phren'o-log'ic-al,** *a.*

A Chart of Phrenology.

1 Amativeness · 2 Philoprogenitiveness ; 3 Concentrativeness ; 3 *a* Inhabitiveness ; 4 Adhesiveness ; 5 Combativeness ; 6 Destructiveness ; 6 *a* Alimentiveness ; 7 Secretiveness ; 8 Acquisitiveness ; 9 Constructiveness ; 10 Self-esteem ; 11 Love of Approbation ; 12 Cautiousness ; 13 Benevolence ; 14 Veneration ; 15 Firmness ; 16 Conscientiousness ; 17 Hope ; 18 Wonder ; 19 Ideality ; 19 *a* (Not determined) ; 20 Wit ; 21 Imitation ; 22 Individuality ; 23 Form ; 24 Size ; 25 Weight ; 26 Coloring ; 27 Locality ; 28 Number ; 29 Order ; 30 Eventuality ; 31 Time ; 32 Tune ; 33 Language ; 34 Comparison ; 35 Causality. [Some raise the number of organs to forty-three.]

Phrenology skull model *(Wikipedia)*

abilities, behaviors, personality, and intelligence. More specifically, Gall's followers claimed to be able to evaluate 35 "faculties" (powers of the mind) and to tell their clients whether their faculties were over- or underdeveloped. The faculties included such traits as conscientiousness, self-esteem, spirituality, friendship, and apprehensiveness. Gall's colleague Johan Spurzheim (1777–1832) took phrenology to the United States, where Orson Fowler (1809–1887) and his brother Lorenzo Fowler (1811–1896) essentially franchised phrenology into a kind of chain-store business. They sold phrenology kits—phrenology charts, books, manikin-like heads, and other paraphernalia— to "examiners" who traveled across America providing advice on which faculties people should try to strengthen (or control). Although many phrenology practitioners no doubt believed in their product and genuinely intended to provide a useful service, the approach did not generate empirical data, and phrenologists tended to ignore evidence that contradicted their beliefs.

An approach to human understanding that was in many ways similar to phrenology was **physiognomy**, the use of facial features (nose, chin, eyebrows, forehead) to analyze personal intelligence, character, and personality. Although the idea of physiognomy dated from the Greeks, Swiss theologian Johann Kaspar Lavater (1741–1801) popularized it in the late 18th century. Like phrenology, physiognomy lacked scientific foundations, but nevertheless persisted until the early 20th century, and actually played a role for a time in selection of workers in America. One of the more interesting historical applications of physiognomy could have profoundly changed the face of science: Charles Darwin (1809–1882) reported that he nearly lost the opportunity to make his historic scientific voyage aboard the *H.M.S. Beagle* because captain Robert FitzRoy, a believer in physiognomy, thought the shape of Darwin's nose suggested he would lack the determination and energy required to make the trip. Darwin's case illustrates the danger of the unfounded conclusions, including bias and stereotypes, inherent in these pseudoscientific approaches to understanding human behavior.

FOUNDATIONS OF A NEW SCIENCE

Following Newton and Locke, serious thinkers of the 17th and 18th centuries began to believe that the route to understanding lay not in the authority and dogma of the past, but in the methods of reason and science. This era came to be called the *Enlightenment*, and led not only to empiricism and associationism, but to a widespread acceptance of critical thought and intellect. It was an optimistic era, characterized by belief that the world was naturally improving, and by important advances in political thought and economics, as well as science. The growing prestige of science, and the increasing acceptance of the idea that scientific observation could unlock nature's secrets, lasted well into the 19th century; and it is then that the story of modern scientific psychology truly begins.

Specific Nerve Functions

Johannes Müller (1801–1858) was a brilliant young German scholar, completing his medical school studies at the age of 21. By his mid-20s he had written important books about the physiology of vision, and was teaching anatomy and physiology to university students. His many discoveries and accomplishments led to his recognition as the father of scientific methods in German medicine. Despite several bouts of crippling depression and his premature death (probably by suicide) at age 57, Müller made one fundamental contribution to the field that would become especially critical to physiological psychology: the law of specific nerve energies. This idea, which Müller published in 1826, held that the nerves serving each sensory system could carry only one type of information. Thus, auditory nerves could carry only sensations for sound, optic nerves only sensations for light, and so forth. This doctrine stood in contrast to the earlier belief that any nerve could carry any kind of sensory information to the brain. And although other scientists had previously proposed similar ideas, it was Müller who demonstrated, publicized, and made the specific nerve energy law a part of the accepted body of science. In so doing, he set psychology on the path to answering one of its important questions: How does the physical reality of the environment become perception in the mind (brain)?

Understanding the Nerve Cell

The movement toward scientific explanation of human experience and functioning led to the formation of a group of young German scientists in 1845. Known as the Berlin Physical Society, the members of this group believed they could understand the nervous system and mental processes via physical principles. One member of the society, Hermann von Helmholtz (1821–1894), would become one of the great scientists of his (or any) time. Although he would later establish himself as one of the most important figures in the study of vision and hearing, one of his greatest contributions to the science of psychology came in the early 1850s.

Scientists at the time realized that nerve impulses involved electricity, but they did not fully understand how nerve cells worked or how fast nerve impulses could travel. They assumed that if the process was electrical, nerve signals would travel too fast to measure, possibly at the speed of light. It was Helmholtz's colleague and friend Emil du Bois-Reymond (1818–1896) who found that the firing of a nerve cell (**neuron**) involves both a chemical reaction and an electrical impulse, leading to the term we use today to describe the process: **electrochemical**. This discovery led Helmholtz to think that perhaps nerve signals did not move with the speed of electricity, and that it might be possible to measure the transmission time. Using muscle and nerve from a frog leg, he was able to demonstrate that nerve impulses not only travel at measurable rates of speed, but that the rate is nowhere near the speed of light. The average speed, Helmholtz found, was about 90 feet per second. When he then studied nerve impulse speed in humans, he found a range of about 165–330 feet per second (about 100–200 mph). When Helmholtz published his findings in 1850, others did not believe them at first; but his data could not be refuted, and his work profoundly changed the future of experimental psychology.

Mapping the Brain

Müller discovered specific *nerve* functions. Could it also be true, other researchers wondered, that specific areas of the *brain* might also have very specific functions? (Gall had made this argument, but was wrong about the details) A tragic accident that occurred in Vermont in 1848 provided a few early answers. While working on a railway construction site, Phineas Gage accidentally ignited blasting powder that drove a large tamping iron (a metal bar) through his skull. The tamping iron entered below his left eye and exited through the top of his head. Remarkably, this accident was not fatal, although Gage lost part of the left **frontal cortex** of his brain. Although Gage recovered, his behavior changed significantly following the accident. Previously, according to one of his doctors, he had been intelligent, well adjusted, and a persistent planner; after the injury, he used gross profanity and was impatient, insensitive, and irreverent. His behavioral and personality changes were permanent, lasting until his death 12 years after the accident—suggesting dramatic effects of injury to a specific brain area.

About the time of Phineas Gage's death, a French doctor, neurologist Paul Broca (1824–1880), was studying a long-term hospital patient known simply as "Tan." Broca called him Tan because, although the patient understood what other people said to him, his response was always to gesture and say "tan, tan."

Phineas P. Gage *(Wikipedia)*

Tan had a condition called **expressive** (or motor) **aphasia**—meaning that he had normal intelligence and understanding and could speak, but could not form and express ideas in his speech. When Tan died, Broca examined his brain and found a damaged area in the left frontal lobe. After studying more patients with similar aphasia, Broca concluded that this small frontal lobe region in the left **hemisphere** was a primary location for speech, adding more evidence to the argument for specific functions of brain areas. In recognition of his discovery, we now call this particular part of the brain **Broca's area.**

Soon after Broca's discovery, a parallel finding came from the work of German doctor Carl Wernicke (1848–1905), who worked with a group of patients who could speak normally, but whose speech content was nonsense. These people also lacked the ability to understand language, and all of them had damage to a different area (now called **Wernicke's area**) not far from Broca's area in the left brain. In 1870, two other Germans, Eduard Fritsch (1838–1927) and Edward Hitzig (1838–1907) reported research in which they electrically stimulated the brains of dogs, identifying a strip along the midbrain that controls motor movements—what we now call the **motor cortex**. Other investigators began identifying other brain areas with specific functions, and by 1876 Scottish researcher David Ferrier (1843–1928) had published a map of the monkey brain showing the role of a variety of brain areas. These 19th-century scientists were well on the way to establishing the localization of brain function—an area of study that continues today through use of such technologic advances as **positron emission tomography** (PET) scans and **functional magnetic resonance imaging** (fMRI).

A NEW SCIENCE IS BORN

A number of scholars could have laid claim to the title of founder of the field of psychology. For example, David Hume wanted to see a "science of man," David Ferrier produced a brain map, Johannes Müller and Hermann von Helmholtz extended understanding of how the nervous system works, and the German Gustav Fechner (1801–1887) brought together physiology and physics in his **psychophysics** to demonstrate the potential of experimental study of psychological phenomena. Some might also argue that the founder could be Hermann Ebbinghaus (1850–1909) who, working in the 1870s, conducted groundbreaking research leading to a fundamental understanding of memory, which remains relevant today. Ebbinghaus, however, had no real laboratory and did not publish his work until 1885. It remained for another German scientist to mark the generally accepted birthday of modern psychology.

The First Laboratory—Wilhelm Wundt

It was a December day in 1879 when Wilhelm Wundt (1832–1920) and two students, a German named Max Friedrich and an American named G. Stanley Hall, quietly set up the equipment and instruments for an experiment in a small room in the *Konvikt* building—a structure built by prisoners—at the University of Leipzig. This date is generally accepted as the time when a psychologist first used a laboratory for a truly experimental purpose (as opposed to using a lab for teaching demonstrations). Psychology thus had not only a subject matter, but also, for the first time, a place clearly set aside for psychological research. Wundt even called the lab the *Psychologisches Institut*. Wundt was well familiar with the scientists who came before him; he had studied and worked, for example, with both Müller and Helmholtz. He had also studied with Robert Bunsen, inventor of the well-known Bunsen burner, which you may have seen in a high school or college chemistry laboratory. Connections aside, however, we consider Wundt to be modern psychology's founder not only because he established a laboratory but mostly because of his important research, writing, and teaching.

Indeed, one of Wundt's most enduring contributions to the field came before the founding of his laboratory. In 1874 he published *Principles of Physiological Psychology*, announcing his intention to establish the boundaries of a new science, a science that we would today call *experimental psychology*. Wundt was interested in the study of immediate conscious experience—a phenomenon that he attempted to investigate by carefully training individuals in experimental self-observation. His laboratory was also home to experiments investigating many other things, including reaction time and perception of visual stimuli (color, intensity, duration) and auditory (sound) stimuli. Wundt also established a journal, *Philosophical Studies*, to provide a place for many of these studies to appear in print.

Wundt actually developed two differing points of view in psychology. The first, which was called **voluntarism** and was based on his interest in immediate experience, held that conscious experience has two aspects: the content of the experience itself and the interpretation given the experience by the individual (what he called "apprehension"). It was the latter that Wundt found particularly interesting, and he believed it could be studied via experimental methods. The second important perspective was something Wundt called *Völkerpsychologie* in the 10 volumes he wrote under that title over a 20-year period. Today, we might call this **sociological psychology** (see Chapter 8). Important within the legacy Wundt left the field are the ideas that psychology should rely on observation, that it requires internal explanation, and that the nature of humans is knowable through scientific methods. Wundt attracted students from across the continent of Europe as well as many from America; he eventually served as advisor for more than 180 doctoral students at Leipzig, 33 of them Americans. Several of these Americans went on to become prominent in the field and established some of the very early laboratories of psychology at American universities, including those at Johns Hopkins, Pennsylvania, Columbia, Nebraska, Northwestern, Cornell, and Stanford.

Despite earning recognition as a splendid teacher, Wundt did not leave behind a large number of disciples to keep his theoretical and scientific views alive; as a result, his perspectives on psychology were largely forgotten (or at least forsaken) by the 1920s, replaced by newer perspectives on both sides of the Atlantic. Nevertheless, Wundt remains a giant in the history of the field, a pioneer in experimental methods and a powerful influence on the scholars and scientists who were to define psychology's future.

The Dawn of American Psychology—William James

In 1875, four years before Wilhelm Wundt established his research laboratory in Germany, William James (1842–1910) began teaching the new experimental psychology at Harvard University in the United States. Trained in medicine and widely educated in European schools in several countries, James was fluent in five languages. He once joked that the first psychology lecture he ever heard was the first one he gave: Except for phrenology and Scottish mental philosophy, before James came on the scene there was no opportunity to study psychology in the United States. James had established a laboratory at Harvard as early as 1875, but he used it for teaching demonstrations not for experimental research, and thus left it to Wundt to get credit for the first true psychology lab.

In 1878 at the urging of book publisher Henry Holt, James agreed to write a psychology textbook. Holt wanted him to finish the book in a year, but James asked for two years. It actually took him 12 years to complete the book—a 1,400-page, two-volume work that was titled *The Principles of Psychology* and became a classic in the field. Remarkably, in the 120 years since its publication, *The Principles* has never gone out of print. Soon after its publication, James produced a shorter version, *Psychology: The Briefer Course.* Before long, students were calling the original volumes "James" and the abridged version "Jimmy!" The book treated

William James *(Library of Congress)*

psychology as a natural science, as the Germans had, but James moved the field in a new direction. He was interested in conscious processes to the extent that they brought about change in the life of the person experiencing them. The **stream of consciousness** as he called it, served a functional role in the person's adjustment to the environment—an idea reflecting the influence of Charles Darwin with his focus on adaptation and biological utility. Consciousness, James believed, evolved as a process useful to survival because it helped people to make good decisions. James's theories played a significant role in the development of a uniquely American psychological viewpoint, **functionalism**, although James did not actually consider himself a functionalist. Nevertheless, it was a movement that defined much of the field in the early 20th century.

Functionalism

Although it was the first truly American system of psychology, functionalism was not a clearly defined perspective. Instead, it was characterized by a rather broad group of psychologists who raised such common questions as what people do and why they do it. The term *functional* has two meanings in relation to this psychological viewpoint. First, the functionalists took seriously (as did James) **evolutionary theory** and the resulting emphasis on the adaptability or usefulness (*functions*) of behavior and consciousness. Second, these psychologists wanted to understand the relations between the antecedents (prior causes) and consequences (outcomes) of behavior—the kind of connection between variables that scientists call *functional* relationships. Along with the practical implications of the knowledge of psychology, individual characteristics and differences were also important to the functionalists.

It was 1896 when John Dewey (1859–1952), then working at the University of Chicago, published an article titled "The Reflex Arc Concept in Psychology." Dewey's article, according to historians of psychology, marked the starting point for functionalism. Physiologists had divided the concept of the **reflex** into three distinct parts: stimulus (creating a sensation), processing (creating an idea), and motor activity (a response). This analysis, Dewey believed, was an awkward, artificial way of thinking about reflexes. He proposed a view of the reflex as a coordinated action integrated with more complex learning activities and a focus on how such activities function to allow the learner to adapt to a changing environment. Dewey made Chicago an early center for functionalism, bringing like-minded colleagues to a department that encompassed philosophy, experimental psychology, and pedagogy (the science of teaching).

Two of Dewey's Chicago colleagues, James Angell (1869–1949) and Harvey Carr (1873–1954), further defined functionalism and its role in understanding the evolutionary functions of consciousness in such areas as development, abnormal behavior, mental testing, and learning. Functionalism also found a home in New York at Columbia University, where Edward L. Thorndike

(1874–1949), a comparative psychologist studying both animals and humans, was active in advancing understanding of the ways organisms adapt to their environments. Thorndike became famous for his work with cats in puzzle boxes—an apparatus requiring confined cats to learn to operate latches to secure their release. An important result of this work was Thorndike's *Law of Effect*, which stated that responses followed by satisfying consequences become connected to the situation, and are more likely to recur when the situation arises again, thus suggesting an adaptive function for behavior. But Thorndike's work extended far beyond the animal laboratory—to psychological testing, educational psychology, and authorship of hundreds of articles, textbooks, and tests, making him one of the most famous of American psychologists. Thorndike's work would also provide an important link, leading from functionalism to the new perspective of behaviorism, which we will explore in the next chapter.

Structuralism

Whereas James and the functionalists were establishing a uniquely American psychology at the end of the 19th century, Edward Bradford Titchener (1867–1927) set out to take the German psychology of Wilhelm Wundt to America. Although he was English by birth, Titchener had studied with Wundt and was temperamentally German. He spoke German fluently, he admired German culture, and he maintained traditionally German behaviors and personality throughout his life. In 1892 Titchener moved to Cornell University in New York, bringing with him an interest in understanding mental experience by analyzing it into its simplest elements. With regard to consciousness, Titchener wrote that he wanted to discover what it was—not what it was for. This made Titchener's position quite different from that of the functionalists, who were interested in consciousness as a useful process. Titchener made the contrast between the two viewpoints clear in an 1898 paper titled "The Postulates of a Structural Psychology."

Titchener thus had no interest in *applied* psychology, arguing instead for a *pure* experimental psychology. He did not consider the study of child behavior or animal behavior properly psychological, believing that experimental scientists should not concern themselves with the application of their work. Instead, Titchener emphasized an approach that had highly trained observers reporting on their own mental processes (such as perceptions). Wundt had required as many as ten thousand practice observations by subjects in his laboratory; Titchener wanted even more. This carefully trained self observation was known as **introspection**, a term with a very specific meaning for both Titchener and Wundt; it was nothing like the kind of informal, reflective thought process that the word introspection more often means today.

Like his teacher Wundt, Titchener used elaborate demonstrations to illustrate and supplement his lectures, and he was author of hundreds of professional publications. And like William James, he was a pioneer in allowing women to study with him. In 1890, James admitted Mary Whiton Calkins (later to be first female president of the American Psychological Association) to a graduate study program with him; unfortunately, Harvard refused to grant doctoral degrees to women at this time. But it was one of Titchener's students, Margaret Floy Washburn, who became (in 1894) the first American woman to earn a Ph.D. in psychology. But Titchener's enlightened views on women and doctoral degrees did not extend to other arenas. Until his death in the 1920s, he refused to allow women to attend meetings of the Experimentalists, a group he had established in 1904. Perhaps deservedly, it was this group's rigid, dogmatic stance, a lack of interest in applications, and its isolation from other points of view that contributed to the death of structuralism. Although he left behind the legacy of an independent science of psychology, Titchener's structuralism essentially died with him, giving way to new perspectives that offered not only the promise of good science but also useful approaches to solve human problems.

CONCLUSION

This chapter provides a background summary of how the field we now call psychology emerged and progressed, from the early interest of philosophers and physicians in mind, soul, and behavior, to a more modern understanding of the role of the nerve cell and the specialized functions of the brain. Along the way, the field emerged from the shadow of physiology, medicine, and philosophy, becoming, in the late 19th century, an independent science with its own methods, laboratories, and practitioners. Like other sciences, psychology has endured the threats of pseudoscientific enterprises, but it has also developed a body of knowledge leading to distinct perspectives and schools of thought. In the coming chapters, we will explore the most important of those perspectives.

CHAPTER 2

BEHAVIORISM: A REVOLUTION IN THE SCIENCE OF PSYCHOLOGY

Although it persisted through the first two decades of the 20th century, structuralism by that time was largely limited to the work of Titchener at Cornell University, and the practical aims of functionalism became increasingly prominent in American psychology. Meanwhile, the work of E.L. Thorndike, reported in 1911, was moving the field toward the experimental study of behavior. Thorndike called his theoretical perspective **connectionism**, emphasizing the connection between behavior and its consequences. As he showed in his **Law of Effect**, when animals (like his cats in puzzle boxes) behaved in ways leading to successful outcomes (escape to food), their behavior was "stamped in." He also found that practice strengthened the connection between stimulus and response—an effect that he labeled the **Law of Exercise**. In his work with animals, Thorndike brought the functional psychology of William James, John Dewey, and their students and colleagues into the psychological laboratory.

THE BIRTH OF BEHAVIORISM: JOHN BROADUS WATSON
While Thorndike was establishing his research program at Columbia, another young scholar, John Broadus Watson (1878–1958), was completing his doctoral research at the University of Chicago. Watson studied with Dewey and the other functionalists, as well as with other faculty in physiology and neurology. He received his doctoral degree, based on his work in animal (rat) behavior, in 1903 at the age of 25—making him the youngest person to complete the Ph.D. at Chicago up to that time. As an undergraduate student at Furman College,

Watson had a reputation as a rebel, and as a scientist he lived up to that reputation. Thus, although he used the venerable E.B. Titchener's laboratory manuals in his teaching for a time, he eventually rejected the role of consciousness in the psychology of both the structuralists and functionalists and moved to Johns Hopkins University in Baltimore, where he was named a full professor at the age of 30, and set about redefining the field of psychology.

In rejecting mentalistic explanations of behavior, Watson described a viewpoint known as **behaviorism** and declared that "Psychology as the behaviorist views it is a purely objective experimental branch of natural science." He published this perspective in 1913, in an article titled "Psychology as the Behaviorist Views It"—a statement that others, in later years, would call the "behaviorist manifesto," in recognition of its key role in announcing

Watson the Troublemaker

It seems likely that J.B. Watson's reputation as a troublemaker was well deserved long before he shook the foundations of the field of psychology. He grew up in rather difficult circumstances, with an alcoholic father who was violent and who left the family when Watson was a young teenager. Unlike his father, Watson's mother was a devoutly religious woman who opposed smoking, drinking, and dancing, and who asked her son to promise that he would become a clergyman. Watson attended rural schools in small towns before his mother moved the family to Travelers Rest, South Carolina, near Greenville. It was there that Watson attended high school—a time he remembered as unpleasant; he was not a good student, and he was frequently in and out of trouble. He was arrested for racial fighting and for illegally firing a gun.

Given his record, Watson did not seem to be a good candidate for college. Realizing this, he arranged to get a personal interview with the president of Furman College in Greenville and somehow managed to be admitted, starting his college career at the age of 16. His interest in the ministry did not last long, but he became an honor student at Furman. However, as Watson told the story, one of his professors, Gordon Moore, promised to fail any student who submitted a paper with the pages backward; when Watson was a senior, he supposedly decided to test Moore, and Moore, keeping his promise, failed Watson. This, so the story goes, required him to stay at Furman for an extra year, eventually graduating with a master's degree in 1899.*

Source: Hothersall, D. 2004. *History of Psychology*, 4th ed. Boston: McGraw-Hill.

*The truth of this story is uncertain; although Watson reported it, Charles Brewer of Furman University has been unable to find any record that Watson ever failed a course there.

to the world this new experimental point of view. And Watson provided a more comprehensive summary of his perspective a few years later in his book *Behaviorism*. In this book he clearly asserted that human *behavior* (not consciousness) is the subject matter of psychology, denounced mind (soul)-body dualism, and argued that the proper interest of behavioral psychology (like other sciences) is to predict and control its subject matter through the use of experimental methods.

Watson believed there was no good evidence for inheritance of important human traits, and that environment—experience and training—would prove the most powerful influence on behavior. To illustrate his point, even though he knew he did not yet have the data to prove it, Watson, writing in *Behaviorism*, declared:

> Give me a dozen healthy infants, well-formed, and my own specified world to bring them up in, and I'll guarantee to take any one at random and train him to become any type of specialist I might select—doctor, lawyer, artist, merchant-chief, and yes, even beggar-man and thief, regardless of his talents, penchants, tendencies, abilities, vocations, and race of his ancestors.

Parents, Watson believed, should learn to control a child's environment in such a way as to ensure development of desirable conditioned reflexes. He went on to conduct studies of the conditioning of emotional reactions in children, and in his *Psychological Care of Infant and Child* provided practical childrearing advice to parents. Although modern child psychologists probably would not agree with some of Watson's advice (don't hug or kiss children, but shake hands with them in the morning, treat them as young adults), much of it was practical, and he certainly recognized the need for effective support and training for parents; in fact, his child care book was dedicated to "the first mother who brings up a happy child."

Due to a series of personal problems, Watson left university life in the 1920s, becoming a successful pioneer in the field of advertising. His interest in psychology continued, however, and with psychologist Mary Cover Jones he carried on work on child behavior. Their research on approaches to overcoming fears in children eventually led to such techniques as **desensitization**, a procedure widely used today for treatment of phobias and fears; it signaled the potential importance of behavioral research that had begun a few years before, across the Atlantic in the Russian city of St. Petersburg.

CLASSICAL CONDITIONING—IVAN PETROVICH PAVLOV
In 1904, a year after Watson had completed his doctoral studies at Chicago, the Russian physician I.P. Pavlov (1849–1936) received a Nobel Prize for his work on digestive processes. In their studies of digestion, Pavlov and his students

Ivan Pavlov (*Popperfoto/Getty*)

observed the function of salivary glands in dogs, noting that the dogs often salivated when they saw objects (e.g., feeding bowls) they associated with food; Pavlov called such objects "psychical stimuli" and thought they would lead to an understanding of the brain. He eventually experimented with a number of **conditional stimuli** (CSs), pairing other "nonfood" stimuli such as the sound of metronomes with food, the **unconditional stimulus** (UCS) that produced a natural response. After a number of pairings of a CS with food, the CS alone would bring forth salivation. In this case, the salivation in response to the CS (in the absence of food) became known as a **conditional response** (CR). This framework, production of a CR through pairings of CS and UCS, formed the basis of a type of learning that we now call *Pavlovian* or **classical conditioning**. Today we know that the classical conditioning mechanism underlies the learning of conditioned reflexes and emotions. It is this process that Watson believed to explain human behavior.

Pavlov counted Charles Darwin, his Russian predecessor I.M. Sechenov, and American E.L. Thorndike among the major influences on his work, and he was careful in his methodology. For example, **replication**—the repeating of scientific studies to verify their findings—was a regular feature of work in Pavlov's laboratory. He also rejected the dualism of mental and physical processes, insisting that scientific study of reflexes should be limited to observable external stimuli and physiological responses that he could measure.

Pavlov and his followers demonstrated a number of interesting and important characteristics of classical conditioning that still guide the research practices of contemporary researchers. For example, after establishing a link between a specific CS and CR, a researcher may then test the same animal with a new stimulus that is similar (but not identical) to the CS first used. If the animal begins to respond to the new stimulus, we say the CR has **generalized** from the original CS to the new one. If, however, the test animal is exposed to the CS (such as a whistle) repeatedly without the associated UCS (such as food), the CR will eventually weaken and fade—an effect known as **extinction**.

Laboratory research continues today on many complex aspects of classical conditioning, and clinical psychologists, following the lead of Watson and Jones, have used their knowledge of classical conditioning to develop a variety of behavior therapies based on such conditioning techniques as desensitization and **counterconditioning**. Pavlov himself, intrigued and impressed by the applied possibilities of classical conditioning, devoted the last years of his life to study of the relation of his work to psychological disorders in humans.

As important as their work was, neither Watson nor Pavlov had fully explained human behavior. The classical conditioning model is powerful, but there are many aspects of behavior that seem neither reflexive nor emotional in nature, and which therefore extend beyond the bounds of the Pavlovian model. Thus, efforts to extend the scope of behaviorism and its ability to explain a broader range of human and animal behavior would dominate the field of experimental psychology for much of the remainder of the 20th century.

BEHAVIORISM'S HIGH PRIEST—BURRHUS FREDERIC SKINNER

Sometimes called a *neobehaviorist* (new, or recent, behaviorist), American B.F. Skinner (1904–1990) became the 20th-century face of behaviorism. Although we will note the contributions of others of his generation, it was Skinner who served both as advocate for 20th-century behaviorism and as lightning rod for its critics. Skinner wanted to go beyond what he called the "push-pull type of causality" implied by the reflex psychology of Pavlov and Watson. He also set an expansive agenda, both for himself and for the field. "The major problems facing the world today," Skinner said, "can be solved only if we improve our understanding of human behavior."

After taking an undergraduate degree in English, Skinner spent two years attempting to become a writer. During this time, he took an interest in Pavlov and Watson, and subsequently began graduate work in psychology at Harvard University, even though he had never before taken a psychology course. Undaunted by his belated interest in the field of psychology, Skinner approached the subject with great confidence. In a letter to a friend, written early in his first year at Harvard (1928), Skinner commented about the likelihood of "making over the entire field to suit myself." And that was what he did. Within a year or two, Skinner had turned his attention to precise control and understanding of rat behavior and had built laboratory apparatus allowing careful study of rats engaged in pressing a lever to produce bits of food. He called the resultant strengthening of the lever-pressing behavior **reinforcement**, noting that much behavior that others had considered spontaneous was in fact controlled by its

The Behaviorist Has a Sense of Humor

Although he was sometimes criticized for being arrogant, insensitive, or self-centered, there is no doubt that B.F. Skinner had a sense of humor. He occasionally showed his humor in ways that also embodied serious efforts to demonstrate the potential of his science. For example, he taught pigeons to compete in a version of table tennis and to play a simple piano; in a televised interview, he raised the tongue-in-cheek question of what a person would do ". . . if you had to choose, burn your children or your books?" You can imagine the uproar he sparked by saying he would burn his children because he was more likely to make a lasting contribution via his books than through his genes.

Skinner had long been an accomplished prankster. In the autumn of 1925, when he was a senior at Hamilton College, Skinner and a friend conspired to advertise a campus appearance by Charlie Chaplin, the great movie actor and director of the silent film era. Skinner and his friend plastered posters around the college and the town, and hundreds of people turned out for the "event," which turned out to be a hoax. College administrators hired detectives to find the perpetrators, threatening to expel them. Luckily for Skinner, he escaped detection, and the story did not come out until much later.

Sources: Bjork, D.W. 1976. *B.F. Skinner: A Life.* New York: Basic Books; Skinner, B.F. 1976. *Particulars of My Life.* New York: Knopf.

outcomes. This was a more rigorous science than that practiced by Thorndike or Watson, and it was different from the work of Pavlov, which had been largely limited to reflexes.

Recognizing that behaviors like lever pressing are *operations* emitted in the absence of clear stimuli (as in the case of reflexive behavior), Skinner called these responses **operant behavior**, and the resulting learning came to be known as **operant conditioning**. Skinner and his colleagues and followers went on to study many ways of arranging reinforcing consequences (**schedules of reinforcement**), leading to improved understanding of how behavior is acquired and maintained.

Unlike other neobehaviorists of his era, Skinner did not consider a complex theory of learning or behavior necessary. He argued for a strictly empirical science, believing that behavior could be understood by careful observation of the external forces (antecedents and consequences) influencing it, and that psychological phenomena could be described in terms of behavior. Thus, he rejected the complex **hypothetico-deductive** (deducing conclusions from theory) approach of Clark L. Hull (1884–1952) and the **purposive** (goal-directed) **behaviorism** of Edward C. Tolman (1886–1959). And unlike E.R. Guthrie

(1886–1959), who thought that all learning depended on the contiguity (closeness in time) between stimulus and response, Skinner considered the **contingency** (causal connection) between behavior and consequence central to behavioral understanding.

Skinner also rejected the typical modes of analysis of the day, which involved statistical treatment of averaged data gathered from groups of subjects; he believed that, with precise control and repeated observations, meaningful data could be obtained from careful study of single organisms. His research results validated his approach, achieving consistency at a level rarely seen in psychological data. Even among those scientists who did not fully agree with Skinner's interpretation of the nature and causes of behavior, his methodological approach, and the kinds of apparatus he developed, became a dominant force in 20th century experimental psychology.

Although Hull and Tolman, along with other neobehaviorists, were popular in their day, it is Skinner whose legacy we remember today in the work he left behind and for its remarkable influence on the many applications of behavioral technology that it spawned. As early as 1948 Skinner wrote a novel, *Walden Two*, describing his vision of a community governed by humane behavioral principles (and anticipating many modern concerns about use of resources and life in concert with nature). In 1953 he published a comprehensive textbook, *Science and Human Behavior*, discussing the application of his science to human beings.

BEHAVIORISM APPLIED

Even as a child, B.F. Skinner had a penchant for building apparatus and using behavioral techniques for applied purposes; at an early age, for example, he built a simple pulley system to remind himself to hang up his pajamas! Soon after beginning graduate study at Harvard, Skinner began developing devices to support his research, and within a few years he had perfected an enclosure for the study of operant behavior in animals—the apparatus that became widely known as the "Skinner Box," and that today remains in use in laboratories around the world. One of the more interesting of Skinner's technological inventions was his Project Pigeon, a World War II-era guidance system that used trained pigeons to direct missiles.

Before long, the technology Skinner pioneered in the Skinner Box found its way into a variety of other applications, first with nonhuman primates, and then, in the 1950s and 1960s, with humans—in the work of Ogden Lindsley with psychotic patients in Boston, of Sidney Bijou with preschool children at the University of Washington, and of Montrose Wolf and Todd Risley with children with disabilities at the Rainier State School. Further work eventually led to the widely known **token economy** program at Anna State Hospital. A program implemented in the 1960s by Teodoro Ayllon and Nathan Azrin, the

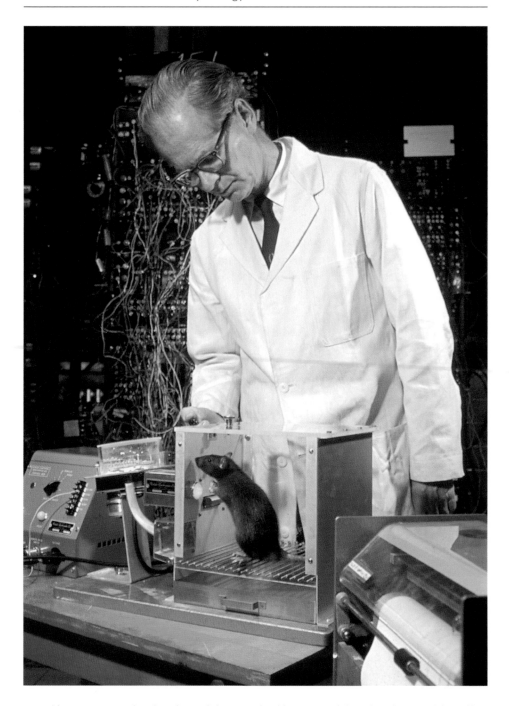

B. F. Skinner at Harvard University, training a rat in Skinner Box. *(Photo by Nina Leen/Time Life Pictures/Getty)*

token economy centered on rewarding desired behaviors with "tokens" that could then be exchanged for something desirable (e.g., food, privileges, merchandise). The program's aim was treating symptoms of mental illness as a set of behaviors that could be influenced— like any other behavior—by their consequences: Patients earned points, or tokens, for engaging in pro-social behaviors and exchanged the tokens for desired objects or activities. This groundbreaking work influenced many other researchers in the field to implement similar programs in other psychiatric settings, classrooms, programs serving people with intellectual disabilities, and in prisons and reform schools. **Behavior modification**—the application of Skinnerian principles to teaching and behavior change in a variety of settings—became ubiquitous.

Among his numerous interests and innovations, Skinner worked to develop teaching machines based on the use of careful analysis of behavior and reinforcing feedback. Others picked up the ball and ran with it. In the hands of Skinner's lifelong friend Fred S. Keller (1899–1996), behavioral technology produced a **personalized system of instruction** (PSI). Often called simply the Keller Plan, PSI was used to improve the way students learned, from early childhood to university courses. Behavior principles also became the foundation for a variety of approaches to effective parent training (a development foreshadowed by Watson's early work), for numerous self-control goals (stopping smoking, weight loss, elimination of tics, and a host of other undesired habits), and for management of people and production in organizations. In 1968, individuals interested in furthering research in the application of behaviorism to problems of social interest established the *Journal of Applied Behavior Analysis*. The revolution had truly begun.

Perhaps the most ambitious and committed efforts to apply Skinner's form of behaviorism came from people who literally sought to achieve a better life. Using Skinner's novel *Walden Two* as a blueprint, a number of groups, beginning in the late 1960s and early 1970s, formed communities based, to varying degrees, on behavior principles. Skinner's aim in *Walden Two* was to create a community that minimized the problems of politics, gender, ownership of property, religion, and childcare by using principles of reinforcement to maximize cooperation, productive use of leisure time, and escape from oppressive values—all in pursuit of the Good Life. Numerous such communes came into being, the two best-known being Twin Oaks, established in 1967 in the American state of Virginia, and Los Horcones, founded in 1973 in northern Mexico. These longstanding communities (both survive to this day) differ from one another, each attempting in its own way to develop a sort of Skinnerian system of behaviors leading to a happy, successful existence and a way of life that people can sustain in harmony with nature and with one another.

Behavior Modification: A Curious Application

In 1969, B.F. Skinner arranged for the republication of a much earlier application of behavioral technology. It was a brief report, written by Benjamin Franklin, which described a practical behavior problem encountered by the early colonial American military. Despite the exhortations of a serious-minded chaplain, the men were not attending daily prayers. Franklin, observing this, came up with a simple behavioral solution.

At the time of enlistment, Franklin pointed out, the men were promised payment, necessary supplies, and a daily ration of rum. They typically received half their rum in the morning and half in the evening. Noting that the men were quite reliable in showing up to collect their rum, Franklin suggested that the chaplain take charge of the distribution of the rum—and that he give it to the men right after prayers. The result was that prayers were "generally and more punctually attended." This, Franklin observed, was a better approach than punishing the men for nonattendance. It is possible this may be the first written report of a deliberate application of reinforcement to change human behavior!

Source: Franklin, Benjamin. 1969. Operant Reinforcement of Prayer. *Journal of Applied Behavior Analysis*, Vol. 2: 247.

THE LEGACY OF BEHAVIORISM

By the end of his life, Skinner was the best-known psychologist in the world. Along the way, he had achieved something quite unusual for scientists—celebrity status, which included being featured on the cover of *Time* magazine in 1971. As psychology historian L.T. Benjamin, Jr., observed, ". . . Watson called for psychology to come to the altar of behaviorism, to cast out its demons of mentalism and instrospection. In B.F. Skinner, he found his high priest." But even at the height of Skinner's influence and celebrity, the field of psychology was once again beginning to shift—this time, away from the Skinnerian focus on strictly observable behavioral events and toward the emerging field of **cognitive psychology.** This new trend was gaining support from many psychologists, a significant number of them sympathetic to behaviorism but also wanting to know more about what was inside the "black box," as they sometimes called the human mind. Skinner resisted this trend, almost literally to the end of his life—little more than a week before his death at age 86, he delivered an address condemning the mentalistic nature of cognitive psychology, concerned to the very end about the rise of an approach he saw as lacking science. What, then, is the legacy of behaviorism in general, and of B.F. Skinner in particular?

Because the foundation of Skinner's behaviorism was the strengthening of desirable behaviors and the weakening or elimination of undesirable ones, his psychology has found application in virtually every facet of the discipline. For example, the development of behavior modification (or **behavior therapy**) brought effective new techniques to the field of clinical psychology, along with strong standards for evaluation or proof of that effectiveness. These standards, even in the hands of therapists who would not consider themselves behaviorists, have remained a central feature of the work of many clinical and counseling psychologists. And although the token economy is virtually a thing of the past, its departure from the scene occurred not due to lack of effectiveness (in fact, the approach was extremely effective), but due instead to changes in treatment philosophies that dramatically restructured the face of treatment and service delivery. In the field of intellectual disabilities, for example, large institutional settings have essentially disappeared, in favor of smaller community-oriented services; and those services, in deploying effective training and treatment plans, rely on behavioral techniques and data to plan and assess their work—a state of affairs that did not exist prior to the behavioral revolution.

Also within the realm of clinical psychology, we have previously noted that some important treatment techniques derived from Pavlov's classical conditioning. These have included systematic desensitization (a procedure still commonly used to alleviate anxieties, fears, and phobias), conditioning treatment of bedwetting (first reported in 1928), and treatment of alcoholism.

Behavioral technology has also found a place in industry. Analysts have observed that so-called "Monday morning blues" are much like the **post-reinforcement pauses** Skinner observed in laboratory animals subjected to interval schedules of reinforcement, and workplace managers have used reinforcement techniques to improve safety. Airlines have also used behavioral applications, in improving the packaging of freight and in design of frequent-flier programs.

Behavioral psychology is well entrenched in education, from its use in the design and implementation of special education programs serving hundreds of thousands of students, to the specification of behavioral outcomes in university courses. Behavior analysis has its own division within the American Psychological Association, as well as numerous scientific and professional journals devoted to reporting the work of behavioral researchers.

Thus, the technological legacy of behaviorism is alive and well. So too is the laboratory tradition of the behaviorists, in the conditioning and learning work conducted in nearly all major American universities. And, to the extent they define their concepts in objective, behavioral terms and make careful empirical measurements, most of today's psychological researchers are methodological behaviorists. It would be safe to say that behaviorists have realized the aims of their earlier functionalist colleagues to establish a psychology that achieves relevant application to the real problems and interests of ordinary people outside the laboratory.

CONCLUSION

Behaviorism as we know it today has its roots in the earlier American functionalist movement, and in the research of the Russian physiologists. As I.P. Pavlov was moving from purely physiological experiments and observations to explore the behavior we call reflexes, so too was J.B. Watson emerging from the functionalist tradition to an insistence upon an objective, empirical science of behavior. Like Pavlov, both Watson and E.L. Thorndike took their interests to the animal laboratory.

But it remained for B.F. Skinner to shape the perspective that would truly create a science of behavior, and in the process virtually remake the field of psychology. His work stimulated a revolution, both in laboratory apparatus and procedure, and in the application of psychological principles to important applied problems. Although behaviorism as Skinner defined it has fallen out of favor with some contemporary psychologists (who generally favor more cognitively oriented approaches), his methods persist in the laboratories of most American universities, and a significant number of psychological researchers continue to agree with Skinner's assertion that the field should not abandon the scientific analysis of behavior.

CHAPTER 3

THE ROOTS OF PERSONALITY THEORY: PSYCHODYNAMIC PSYCHOLOGY

The behaviorists believed that what you see is what you get—that those aspects of humanity that matter most are the behaviors we can observe or measure in explicit, objective ways. But this has certainly not always been the case. Many psychologists, especially those interested in understanding human personality, have often used very different approaches to study their subject matter. The most famous of these psychologists, of course, was Sigmund Freud (1856–1939), the father of psychoanalysis.

SIGMUND FREUD: PROBING THE DEPTHS

Born in Moravia, at age four Freud moved with his family to Vienna, Austria, where he was to stay for almost eight decades. It was only in 1938, about a year and a half before his death, that Freud left Vienna for London. He was reluctant to go, but Nazi troops had come to Austria, raided his home, and burned his books—all due to his Jewish roots. Freud was philosophical about this and wrote, "What progress we have made. In the Middle Ages they would have burned me. Now they are content with burning my books." Although he found it hard to believe he was in danger, Freud nevertheless finally agreed to go to London.

By the time he went to London, Freud was world famous. In fact, he was so well known that he sometimes received letters addressed only to "Freud, London." What made Freud famous, of course, was his psychoanalytic theory of personality, a point of view he had spent several decades developing. The

Sigmund Freud (*Library of Congress*)

psychoanalytic school of thought dates from 1895, the year Freud and Josef Breuer published their *Studies on Hysteria*. Freud's career and the development of psychoanalysis coincided in time with some of the other viewpoints of people discussed earlier in this text. Freud's life overlapped, for example, with those of William James, E.L. Thorndike, John Dewey, I.P. Pavlov, John Watson, Edward Titchener, and B.F. Skinner.

While a medical student at the University of Vienna, Freud met Josef Breuer (1842–1925), who would later prove to be an important influence on Freud's work. And following medical school, Freud also met French neurologist Jean-Martin Charcot (1825–1893), with whom he studied in Paris and who influenced Freud's interest in hypnotism and his view of sex as a motivating factor in personality. His friendship and work with Breuer led Freud to take an interest in Breuer's most famous case, the patient known as Anna O.

The Talking Cure

Anna O., whose real name was Bertha Pappenheim, was a young woman who had nursed her beloved father during an illness, but who herself became bedridden in the face of symptoms Breuer considered "hysterical": paralysis of her right side, difficulty in speaking, hallucinations, and loss of appetite, among others. (The term hysteria comes from a Greek word meaning "uterus"—note the similarity to the word "hysterectomy"—and analysts originally thought the disorder was limited to women.). Thus, Breuer and Freud called Anna's complex of symptoms **hysterical**. Breuer saw Anna on a daily basis for a year or more; he probably gave her the pseudonym "Anna" at least in part because she was a friend of Freud's fiancée, and Breuer wished to be sensitive about her identity. Using hypnosis, Breuer induced Anna to remember and discuss, one by one, the circumstances under which her symptoms had started. In this way, Breuer said, she was able to overcome the symptoms. Anna called this approach "chimney sweeping," and the "talking cure" (a term that sometimes continues in use today to refer to psychotherapy). Anna's case also gave us another Freudian term; she had loved her father, and near the end of her treatment she appeared, Freud thought, to transfer her affection to Breuer, her therapist. Freud called this phenomenon, the redirection of feelings toward someone in the past to the therapist in the present, **transference**.

Breuer believed his patient's symptoms to be the result of built-up emotions and that these were relieved through the **catharsis** (release) achieved by therapy. Anna reported, for example, a dream in which she could not use her right arm to protect her father from a snake—resulting in emotional trauma and paralysis of the arm. Although follow-up later revealed that the talking cure did not produce permanent relief of Anna's problems (Bertha Pappenheim was to be in and out of hospital care several times), the case became famous and appeared as the first case in *Studies on Hysteria*. Anna went on to a successful life—she became, in fact, one of the people who founded the field of social work.

Free Association

After learning from Breuer about Anna O., Freud himself encountered a patient whom he called Frau Emmy von N. She was a 40-year-old woman who reported

Sigmund Freud at Home

Freud arrived in London on September 27, 1938. It had not been easy. Escaping the Nazis required payment of a "tax" that amounted to a ransom, and the intervention of both the British and American governments on his behalf. Freud's friend and biographer Ernest Jones helped the family to find their new home in a comfortable house at No. 20 Maresfield Gardens. The house is now open to visitors, and boasts a collection of Freud's books, his famous couch, 10,000 letters, and various artwork and archeological objects he collected. It is furnished very much as it was when Freud lived there with his family at the end of the 1930s.

Visitors can also view home movies of Freud with pets and children and stroll in the garden he very much loved, faithfully maintained to look today much as it did during the time he spent there. When his health failed, Freud's family placed a bed in his study, from which he could see the garden. This is where he died on September 23, 1939. Sigmund Freud's daughter Anna Freud (1895–1982) established a children's clinic in the neighborhood and lived in the house until her death.

Source: The Freud Museum: http://www.freud.org.uk/about/garden/

a variety of symptoms, including hallucinations, facial tics, involuntary noises produced by her mouth, and fears of people. In the course of his work with Frau Emmy, Freud realized that if he allowed her to talk freely about whatever came to mind, she revealed memories that had been previously inaccessible or hidden. This was the technique he came to call **free association**, an approach he discovered made hypnosis (which he had learned with Breuer and Charcot) unnecessary as a tool to induce memory.

Freud also found, however, that some patients could recover memories only with great difficulty or not at all, particularly if those memories were painful, shameful, or otherwise the kind of thing most people might like to forget. These people, Freud came to believe, were protecting themselves from psychological pain—**repressing** their memories or impulses—and although he found that patients usually did not directly recover such painful memories, their free associations, if he allowed them to come out slowly, could overcome **resistance** and lead to the hidden memory or meaning behind the pain. It was this process of working through associations toward the source of conflict that Freud would later call **psychoanalysis** (a term Freud coined during the 1890s).

Dream Analysis

Freud noticed that he often remembered his own dreams in very detailed ways. When he tried to apply the free association technique to dreams, he concluded that they could be analyzed in the same way as other experiences, including hysterical symptoms. He thus believed that dreams contained some material that was immediate, obvious, and available to memory and conscious awareness—what he called the **manifest content** of dreams. For Freud, the manifest content was similar to hysterical symptoms, in the sense that it was the visible indicator of underlying causes or conflicts. Other dream material, in his opinion, was unconscious, anxiety-causing, and subject to resistance. This material Freud labeled **latent content**, which was discoverable through free association.

The manifest content of dreams, according to Freud, symbolized in a safe manner the underlying troubling or anxiety-provoking conflicts that were painful or taboo. Thus, deeper conflicts or wishes, troubling in their nature, lay beneath the apparently harmless manifest level. The interpretation of dreams, Freud said, was the "royal road to the unconscious." Many historians of psychology consider his 1900 book on the subject, *The Interpretation of Dreams*, his most important work.

A Psychoanalytic Theory of Personality

The structure of the mind, according to Freud, comprises three components: the **id**, the **ego**, and the **superego**. The most fundamental of these (and the oldest, according to Freud) is the id. The id includes instincts like aggression and sex; for Freud, it also included everything that is inherited. The id naturally seeks to maximize pleasure and minimize pain, driven by the **libido** (sexual energy). Freud first took the idea of the underlying role of sex from Charcot, and it became a central theme in his ideas. In the Freudian framework, the id operates according to the **pleasure principle**, with no sense of right or wrong, simply seeking to satisfy basic needs for reproduction, aggression, survival, and gratification.

Contrasting with the id (and often in opposition to the id) is the superego. The superego embodies morality, including ethical codes, awareness of the guilt and punishment accompanying violation of moral and ethical guidelines, and the ideals to which we aspire. The superego is largely unconscious, includes the notion of conscience, and often functions to suppress pleasurable activity.

Acting as something of a mediator, the ego develops as children gain experience with the real world. The ego strives to satisfy the impulses of the id, but in ways that are realistic and socially acceptable. It is the ego that allows us to learn to delay gratification, foregoing immediate pleasures in anticipation of longer-term satisfactions. So just as the id operates according to the pleasure principle, the ego is governed by the **reality principle**. Although some psychologists have characterized the ego as the controlling force in personality, Freud saw it as more of a guiding mechanism; thus, as some have suggested, we might think of the ego as something like the rider on a horse. The horse is stronger and provides the energy, whereas the rider attempts to provide direction.

It is the dynamic tension among the structures of personality that gives rise to the term **psychodynamic**, which describes psychological perspectives arising from psychoanalysis. This understanding reflects not only the views of Freud, but also those of his contemporaries and those who came after him. Moreover, as we describe these personality structures, it is important to realize (as Freud did) that they are not structures in the physical or concrete sense. Unlike our brains, hearts, and hands, for example, they are conceptual inventions that help to describe how Freud envisioned personality processes worked. In the parlance of psychological researchers, these personality structures are **hypothetical constructs**—invented intraorganismic (within the person) structures that help explain observed behavior.

A Psychoanalytic Theory of Neurosis

In Freud's personality theory, the ego must be responsive to pressures arising from three sources: the real external environment, the id, and the superego. When the ego cannot cope with these conflicting forces, the result is **anxiety**, and each of the forces has its own corresponding kind of anxiety. Anxiety arising from the id is known as **neurotic anxiety**; from the superego, **moral anxiety**; and from the real, external environment, **objective anxiety**.

It is almost as if Freud saw the ego as under attack. If we extend this metaphor, we can then think about the weapons the ego has at its disposal to fend off that which attacks it. According to Freud, the ego's arsenal against inevitable anxiety was **defense mechanisms**—strategies employed by the ego to control or redirect anxiety by unconsciously distorting reality. The following are some commonly described defense mechanisms:

- *Denial:* The person avoids anxiety or conflict by failing to note, or by disavowing, a painful reality (event, feeling, or thought) that is evident to others. Example: To control unpleasant anxiety about his health, a smoker may deny the relationship between smoking and lung cancer.

Freud Goes to the Movies

At a time when his fee for treating patients was about 20 dollars per hour, Sigmund Freud received an offer from Samuel Goldwyn, the famous American movie maker at MGM. Goldwyn was willing to pay Freud $100,000 to serve as consultant for a film featuring famous love stories from history. The first of the stories to be depicted was the affair between Antony and Cleopatra. Freud, however, was skeptical about motion pictures, apparently because he feared that film makers would take advantage of psychoanalysis for sensationalist purposes. He refused to meet with Goldwyn and rejected the MGM offer. Freud also objected when two of his colleagues, Karl Abraham and Hanns Sachs, agreed to help with the making of another film, which was about psychoanalysis and was titled *Secrets of a Soul*. Despite Freud's reservations, *Secrets of a Soul* was a big hit with the film critics of Berlin. Unfortunately, Freud never saw it. It was shown at a Berlin celebration of his 70th birthday, but he was ill and could not attend.

Interestingly, Freud's dislike of motion pictures seems to have been selective. During his 1909 trip to America, Freud spent the evening of September 1 at the movies in New York. He went in the company of fellow analysts Carl Jung and Sandor Ferenczi. At that time, it is likely that he would have seen a series of short-subject silent films, each one running perhaps three to five minutes in length. On another occasion, much later in his life and just before his move to London, Freud was spotted in a movie theater in Vienna. The program that night was an American double feature: a cowboy movie and a crime film!

Source: Sklarew, B. 1999. Freud and Film: Encounters in the *Weltgeist. Journal of the American Psychoanalytic Association*, Vol. 47: 1239–1247.

- *Displacement:* Unacceptable or painful repressed aggressive or sexual feelings are redirected toward an acceptable substitute or target. Example: A child experiencing unacceptable anger toward a parent may lash out at a pet or a sibling.
- *Projection:* An individual experiencing unacceptable or threatening impulses may mask them by assigning them to others. Example: An individual who fears dishonesty in herself may tend to be suspicious of the honesty of others.
- *Rationalization:* An individual uses self-justifying explanations to cover up a painful or threatening unconscious reality. Example: An abused woman tells herself that she stays with her husband because she really does love him.
- *Reaction Formation:* A person disguises or hides painful unconscious realities or anxieties by expressing an opposite emotion. Example: A religious leader who engages in inappropriate sexual behavior may be a vocal crusader against such behavior in others.

Freud posited that the failure of the three components of personality to work together leads to **psychoneurosis**. And in his view of personality development, Freud thought the individual must cope with a series of psychosexual issues. Perhaps the best known instance of this developmental perspective is the *Oedipus complex*—a stage in which young children ostensibly have sexual desires for their opposite-sex parent. This conflict, for normal personality development, must be relieved by identification with the same-sex parent, according to Freud, and failure of this process produces psychoneuroses. However, as we shall see, not all the psychologists who considered themselves psychoanalysts shared Freud's emphasis upon sexual energy and conflict as a driving force.

NEO-FREUDIAN PSYCHOANALYSTS

Sigmund Freud did not take lightly or respond well to the disagreements that sometimes arose between himself and his followers and colleagues. In fact, after his split from some of his most important followers, Freud formed a small, secret group called the "Committee," giving each of member of the group a gold ring. A number of people whose views derived from those of Freud considered themselves psychoanalysts, of course, but nevertheless came to differ with Freud on key issues. Here we will consider the three who are arguably the best known: Carl Jung, Alfred Adler, and Karen Horney.

Carl Gustav Jung

Carl Jung (1875–1961) was among those who believed that Freud overemphasized the role of sexuality. Jung had begun corresponding with Freud in 1906, and at first the letters were cordial, with Jung assuming the role of eager student.

Jung was a Swiss psychiatrist who initially wrote in support of Freud's psycho-analysis and was viewed by Freud as his "crown prince"—the person who would follow Freud as leader of the psychoanalytic movement. In 1911, in fact, Freud made Jung president of the new International Psychoanalytic Association; Freud did this, at least in part, because Jung was neither Jewish nor Viennese, and his appointment thus made the association seem more broadly representative than it truly was. (The association was in fact largely Jewish and Viennese, and the Viennese group bitterly opposed Jung's election as president, something made possible only because of strong support from Freud.)

But despite their friendly beginnings, Jung and Freud were destined to part ways. Their differences involved not only disparate professional views, but also differences in personality. Jung believed Freud overemphasized sex. Moreover he began to develop his own views (which diverged from those of Freud), partly to satisfy critics in Zurich, where Jung lived and where increasingly anti-Semitic criticism of Freud had emerged, and partly to promote (among other things) his theories about the **collective unconscious**—the idea that, in addition to an individual unconscious, we also share a collective unconscious, with traces of inherited experiences. Jung eventually called his approach **analytical psychology**, and in late 1912 he wrote Freud a pointedly critical letter, suggesting that Freud treated others like children and that it was likely that Freud himself was neurotic. Freud responded, suggesting "that we abandon our personal relations entirely." This exchange marked the end of their relationship, and in 1914 Jung resigned as president of the International Psychoanalytic Association and sev-ered ties with the group. Carl Jung then embarked on a long, successful career, writing many books and especially influencing the disciplines of literature, reli-gion, art, and history.

Alfred Adler

Jung was not the only important analyst with whom Freud had major differ-ences. Another was Viennese physician Alfred Adler (1870–1937) who became interested in psychiatry after reading Freud's *Interpretation of Dreams*. Like Jung, Adler at first had a close relationship with Freud. In fact, he was one of the early members of a small group called the Wednesday Psychological Society, which met in Freud's office to discuss the theory and practice of psychoanaly-sis. This group became the Vienna Psychoanalytic Society, and in 1910 Freud named Adler its president. Before long, however, the members of this group, like those of the International Psychoanalytic Association, were involved in major disagreements.

Along with other critics of Freud's views, Adler disagreed with Freud's cen-tral emphasis on sexuality. He had been chronically ill as a child and felt infe-rior to an older brother—experiences that no doubt played a role in his view that infants are inherently inferior, and that life involves striving to overcome inferiority and achieve superiority and perfection. He is therefore remembered for the **inferiority complex**, and for placing much more emphasis than Freud on social motives. Adler was also interested in the relationship between birth order and personality; he posited for example, that second-born children, although rebellious and ambitious, were more likely to be better adjusted than first-born or youngest children. Eventually, Adler's views helped to bring about an increased emphasis on consciousness and a decreased focus on sexuality in psychoanalysis, and his views played a significant role in the development of a perspective that came to be known as humanistic psychology (Chapter 4).

Adler resigned as president of the Vienna Psychoanalytic Society in 1911 and formed an alternative group, calling it the Society for Free Psychoanalysis (i.e., freed from Freud). He named the focus of this new group and its underlying viewpoint **individual psychology**.

Adler's break with Freud was bitter and permanent. In fact, Freud biographer Peter Gay characterized their split as mutual hatred. When Adler died suddenly of a heart attack in 1937, Freud was apparently pleased to have outlived his old rival and commented to one of Adler's friends, "I don't understand your sympathy for Adler."

Karen Horney

Although women were not a part of Freud's closest circle of associates, some women did become quite successful within the psychoanalytic camp. One of these was Karen Horney (1885–1952), a German-born analyst who completed her medical training at the University of Berlin in 1913, following up with five years of training in psychoanalysis. She became a faculty member of the Berlin Psychoanalytic Institute and also maintained a private practice.

Although she never actually studied with Freud, as early as 1922 Horney wrote and presented papers critical of Freud's views of the feminine personality, including what she considered an antifeminist bias. Unlike Freud, she believed that many sex differences were produced by social influences, not by biological determinants. In the 1920s and early 1930s Horney continued to publish important criticisms of Freud, arguing that women did not envy the anatomy of males (as Freud thought) but were simply denied the power and cultural opportunities available to men. A central issue for Horney was the **basic anxiety** developing from a child's relationship with parents; she also believed that major conflicts could be avoided in the environment provided by a secure, loving home life.

In 1932, in the face of the changing political situation in Germany, Horney left Europe for the United States, going first to Chicago, and then, in 1934, to New York. She became affiliated with the New York Psychoanalytic Institute—a group strongly influenced by Freudian views—but eventually moved away from these views. In 1941 she established a new organization, the Association for the Advancement of Psychoanalysis, which she headed for the rest of her life.

A Very Non-Freudian Therapist

We have briefly discussed some of the neo-Freudians. But in the 1930s, when Freud and the other psychoanalysts were popular in much of the Western world, at least one psychotherapist on the other side of the world was using a very different approach to solving the problems of patients with neurotic anxiety. In Japan, psychiatrist Shoma Morita (1874–1938) of Tokyo developed a therapy with certain features common to Zen Buddhism (although Morita did not deliberately base his work on Zen). Morita believed that psychoneurotic individuals were overly conscious of themselves and therefore preoccupied with feelings.

Morita argued that rather than focusing on feelings, such patients must accept their worries or suffering. Rather than dwelling on these, patients should learn to take action. The therapy began with a period of bed rest during which a patient was to refrain from talking with other people (as well as from reading or writing) and come to terms with the reality of present circumstances. Then, through increasingly demanding work, the patient would move toward a realistic daily life. The emphasis was on cultivating *mindfulness* and moving from being feeling-centered to purpose-centered. In this way the patient would build character and learn what is controllable and what is not. According to Morita, this would promote purposeful behavior and allow escape from the preoccupation with feelings and worries.

Sources: The TŌDŌ Institute (http://www.todoinstitute.org/morita.html); Iwahara, S. 1963. Oriental Psychology, in M.H. Marx and W.A. Hillix, *Systems and Theories in Psychology.* New York: McGraw Hill, 456–469.

Horney deserves credit for her pioneering feminism, especially as it derives from a new interpretation of psychoanalysis that removed from women the stigma of innate neurosis associated with their sex.

PSYCHOANALYSIS ARRIVES IN AMERICA

Although Karen Horney was prominent among psychoanalysts in the United States, she was certainly not the first. In fact, Sigmund Freud himself was instrumental in helping psychoanalysis get a foothold in America. Soon after the turn of the 20th century, Freud's work was creating increasing interest in the United States. He had published several books, and American psychologists were starting to take notice. Notable among these Americans was G. Stanley Hall, who was both a leading psychologist (having founded the American Psychological

Association in 1892) and president of Clark University. The year 1909 marked the twentieth anniversary of the founding of Clark University, and Hall invited many prominent psychologists to participate in the festivities, including Freud and Carl Jung.

Freud, considered the "centerpiece" of the anniversary agenda, delivered five lectures at Clark. He was well received by the American audience, despite the disapproval of some who considered his emphasis on sex inappropriate. Freud received an honorary degree from Clark, and his lectures were later featured in the *American Journal of Psychology*. While participating in the anniversary festivities Freud was a houseguest in Hall's home, along with Carl Jung and William James. But Freud did not leave with a good impression of America. He did not like the food or the informal behavior of Americans, and he found the language difficult. In fact, he later called America "a gigantic mistake," and the Clark conference was his only visit to the New World. Nevertheless, Freud had a following in the United States, and his theory generated significant attention, both public and professional, in the years following his visit.

Sigmund Freud, G. Stanley Hall, C.G. Jung, A.A. Brill, Ernest Jones, and Sándor Ferenczi. *(Library of Congress)*

After Freud's American visit and the Clark conference, psychoanalysis for a time gained the status of an American school of thought in psychology. For example, within two years of Freud's visit, American analysts had established the American Psychoanalytic Association; soon after they were publishing the *Psychoanalytic Review*, the first of numerous American psychoanalytic journals. Although in scientific circles it would soon be overshadowed by the burgeoning behaviorist movement, the Freudian perspective became a significant influence beyond the fields of psychology and medicine in the United States. Freud's work had an impact on other disciplines, including anthropology, philosophy, and literature, and it became a subject of interest for feminists. Perhaps most notably, psychodynamic thinking and such terms as "defense mechanisms," "unconscious," "complex," "id," "ego," "superego," "Freudian slip," and many more became a part of the fabric of American popular culture.

THE LEGACY OF FREUD AND MODERN-DAY PSYCHODYNAMIC PSYCHOLOGY

By one estimate, biographers of Freud have written more than 100 books about his life, and the chances are good that if you have heard of only one psychologist, it would be Freud. It will come as no surprise then that many authorities in the field have offered opinions about Freud and his work and that his influence has not totally faded from the world of clinical psychology.

Evaluating Freud's Theory

Despite his personal and professional differences with many people in the field, by the end of his life Sigmund Freud had provided the inspiration for a psychoanalytic movement that was international in scope. The International Psychoanalytic Association that he established in 1910 continues today, with more than 12,000 members still conducting therapy. However, just as they did in Freud's time, analysts have their disagreements about how to conduct their therapies and about the importance of sexuality and the unconscious. Freud gets credit, of course, for making popular the idea of the unconscious, as well as for his focus on the importance of early development in the formation of personality. Freud's psychoanalysis has also been a major influence on clinical psychology, both in its therapies and its assessments.

But although he was a towering figure in the field of psychology, Freud continues to have many critics. Scientific psychologists have noted that he drew conclusions about human behavior from a small number of cases in the course of treatment. Thus, Freud did not collect objective data in carefully controlled situations. In fact, it may be an exaggeration to call the material from which Freud worked data at all; he made notes after seeing patients, relying on his own memory and note taking to gather information. This procedure, coupled with the potential unreliability of patient self-reports, and the fact that we cannot know exactly what Freud did or said in sessions with patients, makes it difficult to assess his observations and conclusions. (Contrast this with the insistence of Watson or Skinner on the use of objective, observable behavioral data.) The result is a theory that many scientists believe to be built upon shifting sands and a lack of empirically testable scientific propositions.

As the leader of a group of scholars, Freud was often dogmatic and personal in his disagreements with members of the group. As we have seen, he sometimes had bitter disagreements with other scholars and became estranged from people whom he saw as disloyal to his point of view. This, his critics point out, is not the way a scientist interested in fair-minded, objective tests of theory should behave. A number of research projects have attempted to evaluate various aspects of Freud's system, with mixed results. However, both Freud's followers and his opponents would agree on at least this conclusion: His ideas have found their way into all aspects of Western culture, influencing everything from literature to politics and marketing. They have also given rise to a variety of psychodynamic therapeutic approaches that remain in use today. For better or worse, Freud made himself a fixture of modern culture.

Current Psychodynamic Psychology

Psychodynamic theory and therapies have changed in significant ways since the days when Sigmund Freud was seeing patients in Vienna. For example, in Freud's time, children were the subject of analysis only to the extent childhood existed in the memories of adults. Later therapists, including Anna Freud (Sigmund Freud's daughter), extended treatment to children. Their methods have changed appropriately to account for the behavior and needs of children and adolescents and now include such approaches as play therapy. Therapists today also take an interest in a much wider range of problems and disorders than the early psychoanalysts did, with resulting changes in the techniques of analysis, as well as development of many new techniques. Thanks to the early work of such analysts as Otto Rank (1884–1939), therapy is typically much briefer than Freud would eventually have envisioned (although in the early years, Freud thought therapy should be more active and briefer than it eventually became). Furthermore, the concept of psychological emergencies (e.g., posttraumatic stress disorder) has also forced adjustments (in scope and procedure) in psychodynamic therapies.

Today we can also see that the interpretations of interest to psychodynamic therapists tend more often to be based on current life events (rather than personal history), and therapists tend to work with patients to identify specific objectives for dealing with the patients' most critical problems. On the other hand, some psychologists still use personality tests based on the psychoanalytic notion of projection; these **projective tests** aim to get at unconscious processes by asking patients to respond to ambiguous (having several possible meanings)

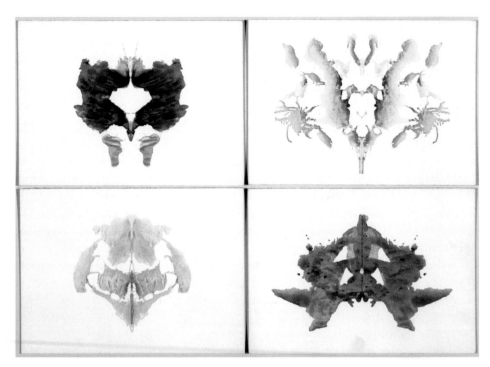

Rorschach inkblot tests.*(SSPL/Getty)*

pictures. The most famous and widely used of these is the *Rorschach inkblot test*, which requires individuals to describe what they see in several inkblots. Finally, we can note that, although the early psychoanalysts were interested in the formative role of the first five years of life, it was psychoanalyst Erik Erikson (1902–1994) who developed a psychosocial (not just sexual) developmental theory that included the entire lifespan.

CONCLUSION

Sigmund Freud is a name known to people around the world. His ideas about the role of unconscious conflict and sexuality in the development of human neurosis revolutionized the field of psychiatry and left a legacy that shaped modern views of psychotherapy. Despite repeated disagreements and splits with friends and colleagues, Freud eventually contributed many concepts and terms to the language and popular culture of the modern world. At the same time, his followers and colleagues, even when they disagreed with Freud, made their own contributions to the field. Initially a European perspective, psychoanalysis came to America early in the 20th century, and Freud himself traveled to the United States to spread his message at the Clark University anniversary celebration.

Although he was a major influence on the field, Freud has not gained as much respect in experimental psychology circles as in the psychodynamic therapeutic community and among scholars in such other fields as literature and philosophy. Scientists see Freud's theory as lacking in solid data and find fault with the experimental testability of its proposals. Nevertheless, his name is a household word, and his place in the history of psychology is secure.

CHAPTER 4

MEASURING THE MIND: INDIVIDUAL DIFFERENCES AND THE BEGINNINGS OF PSYCHOLOGICAL TESTING

By the late 19th century, the work of Charles Darwin and his *On the Origin of Species* was influential in the development of the modern field of psychology. Scientists developed an interest in the similarities and differences between the mental characteristics of humans and other species on the assumption that the human mind evolved from those of so-called lower animals. One of the consequences of this interest, and the accompanying focus on variation among individuals within the same species, was a movement toward the study of **individual differences**. Interestingly, it was Darwin's cousin, Francis Galton (1822–1911) who led the way in this new psychological arena.

However, the idea of testing for individual differences was not a construct that began with Galton. Two thousand years earlier, the Chinese pioneered the use of testing for literacy, verbal ability, and placement of people in official government jobs. Over several hundred years the Chinese debated testing-related topics that would sound familiar to psychologists even today: evaluation of applied vs. abstract skills, social class and test performance, and control of cheating, among others. And Frenchman Paul Broca, whom we encountered in Chapter 1, also examined individual differences, by studying such phenomena as the difference in brain sizes between individuals, between men and women, and across cultural groups. But it remained for Galton to establish the field of individual differences as a formal discipline.

TESTING INDIVIDUAL DIFFERENCES

Francis Galton came from a well-to-do British family, was exceptionally intelligent, and had the luxury and the interest to be able to study a wide range of topics within his field of interest. Among the individual differences that interested Galton (in addition to and sometimes in connection with **intelligence**) were sensory capabilities (sight, hearing, and color vision), height, weight, strength, reaction times, and fingerprints (eventually used by Scotland Yard, the British law enforcement agency). In 1884, at an international health fair in South Kensington, Galton began collecting several kinds of data from people visiting the event; he later moved the exhibit (he called it an anthropometric laboratory) to a museum and continued to study people (17,000 of them) and their individual characteristics.

Galton believed that individual differences, including differences in intelligence, were inherited, a theory he attempted to illustrate in his 1869 work *Hereditary Genius*. This idea prompted his view that humankind could be improved by rewarding procreation by intelligent people and also inspired his interest in the measurement of intelligence. He coined the term **eugenics** (from the Greek for "good birth") to support his idea that British culture should encourage genetic improvement. (Interestingly, Galton himself never had children.) It was Galton's quest for measures of intelligence that led him to collect measurements on the variety of individual characteristics he observed in his anthropometric laboratory. Unfortunately, his belief that these physical and sensory characteristics would be good measures of intelligence did not prove to be true, and it would remain for others to develop useful intelligence tests.

Nevertheless, Galton developed other important measures of individual differences. He was the first to use studies of twins as a way of trying to sort out the effects of heredity and environment, he pioneered the use of surveys, and in 1888 he developed the statistical idea of **correlation** (a measure of the relation between two variables, such as height and weight). And, although his notions about measurement of intelligence did not prove particularly useful, Galton did invent a variety of techniques and devices for recording mental and sensory characteristics. These included such instruments as a photometer for recording color perception, a special pendulum for measurement of reaction time, bottles to collect data on olfactory (smell) discrimination, and of course the Galton whistle.

James McKeen Cattell (1860–1944), the first full-time American student of Wilhelm Wundt (Chapter 1), thought very highly of Galton and went to England to work with him after completing his time at Leipzig with Wundt. Impressed with Galton's anthropometric testing, and with Galton's aim to improve humans through selective breeding, Cattell offered each of his children (he had seven) a reward of $1,000 if they would marry the offspring of college professors! After

Did You Hear That?!

Francis Galton believed that measurement was critical to development of the science of psychology, and he invented a variety of interesting kinds of apparatus to enable collection of data on the sensory and behavioral characteristics of humans and other species. One of the more curious of these instruments was the one that bears his name—the Galton whistle. The whistle consisted of a metal tube that could be adjusted to change the pitch of air flowing through it. A bulb attached to the end of the tube provided the blast of air required to blow the whistle.

Galton developed a version of the whistle that could be attached to one end of a hollow walking stick, with the squeeze bulb attached at the other end. He could then walk the streets of London or the London zoo, adjusting the frequencies of the whistle and observing which animals pricked up their ears, or whether humans seemed to respond. Galton thus found the limits of human hearing, and observed that cats, in particular, were sensitive to high frequencies of sound. A version of the Galton whistle remains in use today—you may know it as a dog whistle.

Sources: Joyce, N., and D.B. Baker. 2009. The Galton Whistle. *APS Observer* Vol. 22 (March); Schultz, D. 1981. *A History of Modern Psychology*, 3rd ed. New York: Academic Press.

returning to the United States, Cattell set up his own program of anthropometric measurement at the University of Pennsylvania; he first used the term *mental test* in an 1890 article published in connection with this program.

Cattell's extensive program included testing memory for letters, strength of hand grip, reaction time, pain threshold, judgment of line length, and timed color naming. Believing that his many measurements would be helpful in identifying talented individuals and that they might be useful in predicting academic ability, Cattell succeeded in convincing the administration of Columbia University (where he had moved in 1891) to allow him to administer his tests to all the incoming students—which he then did for several years. Using the new concept of correlation coefficient (conceived by Galton and refined by Karl Pearson), Cattell and a graduate student named Clark Wissler measured the relation between Cattell's various tests and the Columbia students' grades. To his great surprise and disappointment, Cattell's extensive measurements bore no relationship to the academic performance of the students. Although for practical purposes this result marked the end of the anthropometric testing movement, it certainly did not mark the end of interest in mental testing.

THE BIRTH OF INTELLIGENCE TESTING

In 1881, at about the same time that Cattell first visited Leipzig, the government of France adopted mandatory universal education. And by the end of the century (in 1899), the government was being pressured to allow all children, including those with intellectual disabilities, access to schools. It thus became a matter of some practical importance to develop testing procedures that could identify students with disabilities and provide them with special educational services. The testing programs developed by Cattell and Galton had not produced measures that predicted academic performance, but the French schools now needed such tests.

Alfred Binet

Alfred Binet (1857–1911) had a rather checkered academic history. He had dabbled, unsuccessfully, in research on the effects of magnetism and hypnosis, and he argued (again unsuccessfully) that intelligence could be determined from measurements of the skull and brain size. But he began to rehabilitate his career when, in 1904, he became a member of a French commission to study the problems facing the schools. Binet knew of Galton's research, and he had tried some of Galton's measures on his own children, finding that on most measures they performed much like adults. The exceptions were in the tests that seemed to involve true mental processes—tasks requiring language, thought, and memory. This led Binet to realize that true assessment of intellectual ability would require tests that examined these higher cognitive processes.

THE FIRST IQ TEST

Working with an assistant, Theodore Simon (1873–1961), Binet conducted a number of comparisons between normally developing children and those with intellectual impairments, eventually developing a series of tests that could differentiate between the two groups of students, as well as among students at different age levels. He reasoned that such an age-based approach would allow educators to determine whether a child was performing at age level, or was lagging behind—and if so, how far behind. If a seven-year-old performed at the seven-year level, the child's intelligence would be normal; but if a seven-year-old performed at the five-year level, the child's ability was subnormal. Similarly, very capable children could pass tests at levels above their true (*chronological*) age.

Age, then, was an important aspect of intelligence; this was the origin of the concept Binet called *mental level*, and it led fairly directly to the idea of **mental age**. Comparing a child's mental age (based on the level at which the child could pass the tests) to the chronological age allowed an estimate of the child's intelligence. Before long, a German psychologist, William Stern, had proposed the idea of *mental quotient*, a term that would later give way to the **intelligence** quotient *(IQ)*, a number obtained by calculating the ratio of mental age to chronological age and multiplying this by 100 (to get rid of decimals). Thus, a five-year-old who tested at the five-year level had an IQ of *5/5 X 100 = 100*. On the other hand, a four-year-old working at the five-year level would have an IQ of *5/4 X 100 = 125*. This formula is the origin of the modern-day notion that a "normal" or average IQ is 100.

INTELLIGENCE TESTING GOES ABROAD

Before long, others were developing intelligence tests in the wake of the work of Binet and Simon, and the search was on for improved methods of measurement. Among those who had been disappointed with Cattell's approach in the United States was Henry Goddard (1866–1957). Goddard had established a laboratory at a facility known at the time as the Vineland Training School for the Feeble-Minded (an obsolete term referring to people with intellectual disabilities), and went to Europe in 1908 to visit similar facilities there. Goddard took the Binet-Simon test back to America, translated it to English, and published it as the *Binet-Simon Measuring Scale for Intelligence*.

After testing a large number of people at the Vineland facility, Goddard became a believer in Binet's approach, and he supported the use of the *Binet-Simon* test for identification and classification of people with intellectual disabilities. The existing terms "idiot" and "imbecile," he said, should be used for people with mental ages of one to two, or three to seven, respectively, and it was Goddard himself who coined the term "moron" to refer to people with mental ages between eight and twelve. These labels, of course, are no longer in use.

Taking a Wrong Turn

Unfortunately, Goddard became known not only for the use of intelligence testing, but also for its misuse. In a book titled *The Kallikak Family: A Study in the Heredity of Feeblemindedness*, Goddard purported to show, through an analysis of a family tree, that the family of a woman with intellectual disability had a "good" side and a "bad" side. Goddard attributed the "bad" side of the woman's family to the birth of her great-great grandfather as a result of an affair between a Revolutionary War soldier and a "feebleminded" girl in a tavern. Although his study of the Kallikak family was badly designed and clearly biased, it strengthened Goddard's belief in eugenics, and he argued that "mental defectives" should be institutionalized and should not have children. Involuntary sterilization became, for many years, standard practice in many American institutions, resulting in tens of thousands of sterilizations.

Goddard also became embroiled (from about 1911 to 1914) in a rather scandalous application of the *Binet-Simon* test to immigrants at New York's Ellis Island. Responding to the request of a government official for assistance in screening those arriving at Ellis Island from other countries, Goddard and his assistants selected and tested people whom they believed might give the appearance of "mental defectiveness." They claimed that as many as 80 percent of the people in some ethnic and national groups fell into the "defective" category. As a result, deportations of people who were supposedly "feebleminded" went up dramatically, despite the fact that the people tested were often frightened, uneducated, tired, and did not understand the English-language test (administered through interpreters). And, despite (or perhaps because of) the misuse of testing at Ellis Island, this experience contributed to passage of strict U.S. immigration laws in the 1920s.

The *Stanford-Binet*

Although many had accepted the Goddard translation of the *Simon-Binet* test, Lewis M. Terman (1877–1956) believed the test could be improved by fixing some of the problems of language and structure it embodied. Terman, of Stanford University, was interested in the relative contributions to intelligence of heredity and environment, but believed research questions on the subject would not be answered until improved tests were available. Terman's work with the *Simon-Binet* was not just an improved translation, but a major revision based on work with more than 2,000 Americans, both students and adults. In 1916 he published the test that would be known as the *Stanford-Binet Intelligence Test*, an instrument that has since undergone several revisions, was the first to include the concept of IQ, and is probably the most widely known of intelligence tests. It quickly became the standard tool for the measurement of intelligence and continued in that role for many years.

The Gifted Study

In his original work, Alfred Binet's motivation was to devise a test that would identify children of low ability. Terman, on the other hand, thought it would also be useful to identify special children of high ability. He considered IQ a critically important personal characteristic, and he shared Binet's interest in appropriate classification—he simply wanted to extend it across the spectrum of ability. Terman thus set out to find and test a sample of the most intelligent children in California schools. He eventually tested nearly 1,500 students from elementary, junior high, and senior high schools. Terman found an average IQ of 143 for the high school students, and 151 for the younger students. (Remember that 100 is average.)

Terman's sample was not representative of the population of California school children. It was, for example, more white and middle- or upper-class than the general population. But it did become the most famous and important study of its kind. Terman continued to test and survey this group for the rest of his life (they called themselves "Termites"), and his colleagues followed them through at least the 1980s. The researchers found that, contrary to stereotyped views of *gifted* people, the Termites proved to be professionally productive and successful, healthy, and generally well adjusted. The project established Terman, in the eyes of many, as the father of studies of gifted children.

FROM INDIVIDUALS TO GROUPS

The *Stanford-Binet* test took the field by storm, and it became the model for other tests to follow. Within the first two and a half years after Terman introduced the *Stanford-Binet*, four million American children took intelligence tests. The format of the intelligence tests has varied somewhat over the years, but some, such as the Wechsler series (e.g., *Wechsler Preschool and Primary Scale of Intelligence*; *Wechsler Intelligence Scale for Children*; and *Wechsler Adult Intelligence Scale*), deriving from the work of psychologist David Wechsler (1896–1981), have until the present time maintained content and formats not unlike the *Stanford-Binet*.

The individual intelligence tests were very useful, but they had a significant practical drawback: They required a trained psychologist to administer them to one person at a time. Wouldn't it be useful if a test existed to measure intelligence in groups, with provision for test takers to read their own instructions

The Mother of Gifted Studies

Lewis Terman is justifiably remembered for his important work on the characteristics and the lives of so-called gifted children and adults. But if Terman is the father of gifted studies, Leta Stetter Hollingworth is certainly their mother. While Terman was developing his research on testing at Stanford, Leta Hollingworth was in New York, studying gifted children. As early as 1918, she was teaching a course for the study of gifted children, and in 1926 she published the first textbook dealing with education of gifted children. She had also worked in the public schools of New York City, a leader in the development of school psychology.

Hollingworth was an early supporter of enriched classes for gifted children, and opposed the common practice of simply promoting such students to advanced grades; such promotion, she thought, would take away the advantages of social interaction with a child's age-mates. A leader not only in the area of gifted education, Leta Hollingworth was also an early proponent of women's rights and debunked popular stereotypes of women. Unfortunately, her productive career was cut short by cancer at the age of fifty-three.

Sources: Benjamin, L.T. Jr. 2007. *A Brief History of Modern Psychology.* Malden, Mass.: Blackwell; Goodwin, C.J. 2008. *A History of Modern Psychology,* 3rd ed. New York: John Wiley & Sons.

and record their own answers? This was the challenge facing a special committee of the American Psychological Association when, in 1917, they received the assignment to help the efforts of the United States as it entered World War I. The committee decided that an important contribution would be the creation of psychological tests to quickly classify, based on abilities, large numbers of soldiers. The assignment went to another working group of psychologists, including Terman and Goddard, and was headed by Harvard University psychologist Robert Yerkes.

Working with a group of about 40 psychologists, these researchers needed only about two months to develop two versions of a test they could administer to large groups. The first was the *Army Alpha* test, an exam for soldiers who could successfully complete a written test. For those who could not read, the group developed the *Army Beta* test, based on pictures. The group initially administered the tests in only a few military camps; not long after this, however, the U.S. Surgeon General ordered that the testing scheme be extended to the rest of the U.S. Army. By the end of the war, it had been administered to more than 1.7 million soldiers.

The success of the U.S. Army in developing these group tests was a major contributor to the rise of a massive test development industry. Schools began widespread testing of children, and the intelligence testing movement spilled over into other related areas of ability and individual characteristics: verbal, musical, spatial, mathematical, vocational, and personality. The era also spawned the well-known Scholastic Aptitude Test (SAT). Testing was, in a word, everywhere.

THE REST OF THE STORY

The amazing growth of the testing movement in psychology and related fields is a fact. However, its history has not been all rosy. Individuals such as British statistician and psychologist Charles Spearman (1863–1945) demonstrated correlations among intellectual abilities and suggested that their findings indicated a general intelligence ("*g*") that might well be innate. This argument proved controversial, because studies also showed correlations between school performance and dimensions of intelligence, and critics pointed out that children without access to the learning opportunities of the school environment would be unable to complete many tasks on such tests as the *Stanford-Binet*. Moreover, many questions on the Army Alpha test required information that was clearly not innate and could only have been learned (e.g., questions about sports or politics). Such limitations became particularly evident in the performance of children of ethnic minority groups or impoverished backgrounds.

Another problem arose because authorities like Terman made statements suggesting that ethnic groups (Native Americans, Mexican Americans, African Americans) had inherently lower intelligence than white Americans. In the activist era of the 1960s, critics again assailed standardized testing, arguing that it discriminated racially and culturally—a controversy that continues to this day. In an effort to further explore the multifaceted nature of intelligence, modern psychologists have argued for so-called **multiple intelligences**—as in the eight dimensions set forth by Howard Gardner (linguistic, logistic-mathematical, musical, spatial, bodily-kinesthetic, intrapersonal, interpersonal, and naturalist), the *triarchic* theory of Robert Sternberg (analytical, creative, and practical intelligence), or the contemporary notion of **emotional intelligence** (the ability to perceive, understand, manage, and use emotions).

One thing is sure: Mental testing is not going away. Schools, colleges, organizations, and government all have a stake in ability and intelligence testing, and psychologists continue to conduct research on testing in ever-broadening arenas. The field has changed significantly since the days when Francis Galton went walking at the London zoo with his famous whistle, but psychological testing remains an interesting, controversial topic for psychologists and consumers alike.

CONCLUSION

Although the ancient Chinese discussed what today's psychologists call individual differences, it was Francis Galton, a 19th-century Englishman, who brought the idea of individual difference and intelligence into the modern era. His belief that intelligence (along with many other individual characteristics) was inherited sounds simplistic by today's standards, but he nevertheless contributed to a developing interest in measurement and understanding of intelligence and a number of other human traits. It was a Frenchman named Alfred Binet who developed the first instrument we might today consider an intelligence test, and soon thereafter Henry Goddard brought the test to America, where it was transformed by Lewis Terman into the *Stanford-Binet*.

Testing gained favor in far-ranging applications. It was used with the intellectually disabled, with the academically gifted, and in group formats, such as the military. Despite the misuse of testing in its application to various disabled and ethnic groups, intelligence and how it is measured remain important subject matter for psychologists, educators, and many others. Lively academic conversations related to genetic contribution to intelligence, the definition of intelligence, the question of whether intelligence is learned or innate, and the notion of multiple intelligence continue to spark interest and controversy.

CHAPTER 5

THE HUMANISTIC PERSPECTIVE: PSYCHOLOGY'S THIRD FORCE

Some 20th century psychotherapists believed that psychoanalysts assumed too much of an air of omniscience (knowing everything) and power within the therapeutic relationship. One of these was Carl Rogers (1902–1987), an Illinois native who started his university work with the aim of becoming an agricultural scientist but gave it up after a couple of years to enroll as a student at Union Theological Seminary in New York. Before long, however, he had serious questions about religious doctrine and again changed his mind, this time enrolling at Teachers College at Columbia University to study psychology.

FOUNDATIONS OF THE HUMANISTIC PERSPECTIVE

Although he had respect for scientific methods (and Teachers College had plenty of what Rogers once called "rigorous, scientific, coldly objective" influence), he also studied Freud. But Rogers rejected the Freudian emphasis on unconscious conflict and espoused the idea that the major motivation in personality comes from the individual effort toward **self-actualization**. Self-actualization, the idea that each person has an in-born tendency to realize all of his or her potentialities, was an idea central to the psychology of Abraham Maslow (1908–1970), designated by some historians of psychology as the father of humanistic psychology.

Humanistic psychology, unlike the psychoanalytic perspective, emphasizes an understanding of the healthy person rather than focusing on people with serious psychological disturbances. This is the psychological perspective that gave rise to the so-called *human potential movement* with its emphasis on such personal concerns as lack of meaning, anxiety, and boredom with life. Some writers have called it psychology's *Third Force*, because it presented an alternative to behaviorism and psychoanalysis.

Maslow's Theory of Self-Actualization

After studying the work of other psychologists, including the psychoanalysts who had fled Europe to escape the Nazis, Maslow became convinced that the best models of human nature were people who were making the greatest use of their individual capabilities and characteristics. He considered these people self-actualized, and he studied a small sample of individuals whom he believed had achieved this level of development. He concluded that such people were psychologically healthy, creative and independent, able to objectively perceive reality, dedicated to their work, self-accepting, natural and spontaneous in their dealings with others, and that they had affection and empathy for humanity.

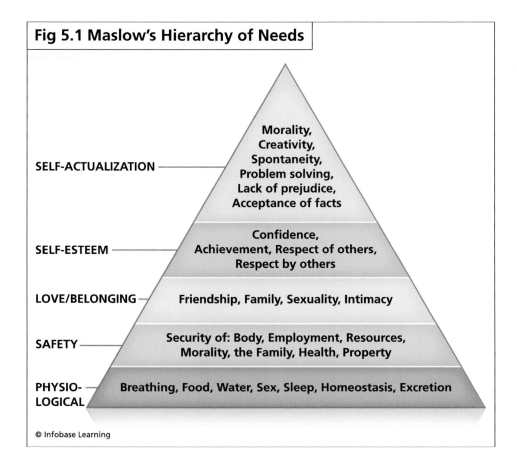

Fig 5.1 Maslow's Hierarchy of Needs

SELF-ACTUALIZATION — Morality, Creativity, Spontaneity, Problem solving, Lack of prejudice, Acceptance of facts

SELF-ESTEEM — Confidence, Achievement, Respect of others, Respect by others

LOVE/BELONGING — Friendship, Family, Sexuality, Intimacy

SAFETY — Security of: Body, Employment, Resources, Morality, the Family, Health, Property

PHYSIO-LOGICAL — Breathing, Food, Water, Sex, Sleep, Homeostasis, Excretion

© Infobase Learning

Self-actualized people, according to Maslow, occasionally had brief episodes of intense wonder, satisfaction, or awe—what he called **peak experiences**.

Although Maslow believed that only a small number (perhaps one percent) of people achieve self-actualization, he nevertheless thought psychology would benefit from studying self-actualization and healthy people rather than focusing merely on the investigation of psychological disorders. To achieve self-actualization, Maslow suggested, individuals must first meet a series of lower (but high-priority) needs: physiological, safety, belonging, and esteem. He saw these needs as hierarchical; that is, physiological needs (e.g., survival, hunger, thirst) are ascribed the highest priority, followed by safety, then the need to be loved and to belong, and so forth. This approach to development and motivation is known as Maslow's **hierarchy of needs**, and appears in virtually every introductory psychology textbook.

Rogers's View of Self

Carl Rogers argued that self-actualization motives underlie the view of the healthy, growing person. His theory of personality depends upon the notion of **self**—those aspects of an individual's phenomenological (experienced) world that the individual sees as "me" or "I." **Phenomenology**, or the study of experience, was, according to Rogers, the foundation for a science of the person. He used the term **self-concept** to describe the totality of the individual's view of self, which included mental, social, physical, and relational characteristics. It is important to note that these notions of self and self-concept were, for Rogers, conscious entities and that individuals experiencing them were fully aware of them—a radical contrast from the way psychoanalysts might use such terms and view such concepts.

Rogers believed that as individuals experience the natural tendency to self-actualize, they form a view of the self-concept they would like to have. Rogers called this aim, the self to which we aspire, the **ideal self**. Thus, the Rogerian view supports two conceptions of self: the one we perceive ourselves to be now and the one we'd like to achieve in the future. We might well ask whether it matters that we have a healthy, positive self-image. The answer appears to be yes. People who have negative views of themselves are more irritable, more critical of others, and more likely to be prejudiced toward others. When our actual self and our ideal self are closely matched, we have a positive self-concept. And, as Rogers posited, if we fail to achieve our ideal self we are likely to be unhappy and dissatisfied.

Existentialism

Writing in the 19th century, Danish philosopher Søren Kierkegaard (1813–1855) set forth a viewpoint that departed from those of previous philosophers, with their focus on human reason and grand, abstract systems of thought.

Who Has a Self-Concept?

Some interesting questions for developmental and personality psychologists concern the concept of self-concept: When do humans begin to be aware of themselves as a distinct entity, and do nonhuman species have the ability to develop self-awareness? Researchers have provided some interesting answers. As early as 1877, Charles Darwin suggested that self-awareness could be checked by observing whether individuals recognize themselves in a mirror, and recent research has shown that human babies may reach out to their own mirror image before one year of age—recognizing the image as another baby. But is this really self-concept? Other studies have used such techniques as daubing a bit of rouge on the baby's nose and then watching. When the baby sees itself in the mirror, will it touch its nose, indicating that it knows "It's me!"? Investigators have found that human children show this level of awareness before the age of two years—sometimes as early as 15 months.

And how about other species? Do they show similar behaviors when faced with images of themselves? In some cases the answer is yes. Chimpanzees, orangutans, and gorillas have shown mirror self-recognition (interestingly, monkeys do not show the same level of ability), as have bottlenose dolphins. These animals show unusual attention, just as children do, to body parts that have been marked or that are not readily visible without a mirror. Does this mean the animals have a self-concept? Opinion is divided on this issue, but it certainly means they have an awareness of self—a capacity that many of us might have assumed was a distinctly human trait.

Sources: Butterworth, G. 1992. Origins of Self-Perception in Infancy. *Psychological Inquiry,* Vol. 3: 103–111; Sarko, D., L. Marino, and D. Reiss. 2009. A Bottlenose Dolphin's (Tursiops truncatus) Responses to Its Mirror Image: Further Analysis. *International Journal of Comparative Psychology* Vol. 15: 69–76.

Instead, Kierkegaard developed a philosophy of the individual, a philosophy which included personal emotions and free will. This became known as a philosophy of existence or **existentialism**. Defining characteristics of existentialism included the importance of the individual and the existence of the individual in the human condition. Like Rogers, Kierkegaard emphasized a phenomenological approach, highlighting each person's unique experience. Also similar to Rogers's view was the existential idea that experience is meaningful only in terms of its significance for the individual—not in relation to any other standard.

According to the existential perspective, it is important that people escape the existential feeling of personal loneliness, that there be others who, through empathy, can be understanding and accepting of the individual. This represents a kind of search for meaning that psychiatrist Viktor Frankl (1905–1997) engaged in during his time in the Nazi death camps of World War II. According to Frankl, humans are the only species that worry about the meaning of their lives, and the will to find meaning is perhaps the most human of all phenomena. Thus, he argued, the role of therapy should be to help patients realize their opportunities and to become what they are capable of being. Although existentialism shares much with humanistic psychology, there is clearly a difference in tone. The humanistic psychologists tend to be optimistic and at least to some extent upbeat, whereas the existential viewpoint is somewhat darker, encompassing human limitations and human tragedy. Psychiatrist Irvin Yalom characterized the difference in cultural terms: Existentialism is a European development, well familiar with a history of war, uncertainty, and geographic limits; humanistic psychology is consistent with the American sense of optimism, limitlessness, and expansiveness.

THE HUMANISTIC PERSPECTIVE AND THERAPY

Therapists in the Rogerian tradition emphasize individual freedom of choice (free will) as a human characteristic of central importance. According to humanistic psychologists, individuals who experience difficulty in using their

No Exit

The name that many contemporary scholars most readily associate with the philosophy of existentialism is that of Jean-Paul Sartre (1905–1980). Sartre, a Frenchman, was both a philosopher and a writer—he is arguably best known as the author of novels, plays, and political material. Although selected to receive the Nobel Prize for Literature in 1964, he declined to accept it, saying he did not wish to be associated with institutions. Sartre recognized the connection between existentialism and the practical concerns of society and politics.

Sartre tried to account for existence using the methods of phenomenology and believed we are free to create ourselves. But, he cautioned, freedom implies total responsibility for our choices, as well as for the anguish, forlornness, and despair that goes with it. It is in working through this suffering, he argued , that we become authentic human beings. It was in his play *No Exit*, first produced in Nazi-occupied Paris in 1944, that Sartre expressed his skepticism of other people, particularly because of their efforts at domination. The most-quoted line from the play is "Hell is other people."

Sources: http://sartre.com; http://nobelprize.org/nobel_prizes/literature/laureates/1964/sartre-bio.html

freedom of choice may be candidates for therapy. The best known therapy in this tradition is Carl Rogers's **client-centered therapy** (also known as **nondirective therapy**).

Client-Centered Therapy

This therapy assumes that the reality experienced by each person is his or her own, and that the individual is motivated to achieve his or her unique potential. However, this actualizing process may be impeded by the *conditional regard* of others. Conditional regard is the sense that others see us as good or worthy only when we act in ways judged appropriate by those others. If parents or other important others impose conditions on their judgment of the worth of the person, that person may deny experiences or behaviors that lead to negative judgments, and as a result, experience a divide between self and reality.

Rogers believed therapists should show **unconditional positive regard**— accepting clients for who they are without judging their worth. Each client, Rogers argued, should direct the therapeutic interaction, with the therapist creating warm, attentive conditions in which the client can make his or her own decisions and exercise the individual capacity for self-growth and self-direction. An atmosphere of respect and unconditional positive regard allows the client to examine the self with confidence. Further, the therapist must recognize and respect the profound responsibility of engagement with a human being who is undertaking the personal struggle for growth and self-actualization—hence the name client-centered. The aim of self-actualization is to become *fully functioning*, which means attaining the highest possible level of psychological health.

Empathy

Empathy is the ability to understand or perceive another person's point of view so that we can share the person's feelings, thoughts, or perceptions. Such empathic understanding, Rogers believed, allowed therapists not only to perceive the nature of the experience of the client, but also to understand the meaning and importance of that experience.

At the level of *primary empathy*, the therapist understands and reflects the client's emotions and thoughts—often restating the client's perspective as a way of demonstrating acceptance and communicating appreciation for the client's point of view. This is essential to establishing unconditional positive regard. But if the therapist is to help the client to move to a new phenomenology, or experience, therapy must go beyond simply reflecting and affirming the client's present perceptions. Such movement may require *advanced empathy*, a process that involves interpretation of the client's thoughts and perceptions; the therapist may, based upon multiple sessions with the client, use his or her understanding of the client's experience to suggest hypotheses or suggestions intended to help the client make decisions about personal change. The idea here is to create conditions for the client to construct a new phenomenological or experiential situation—not for the therapist to impose goals upon the client.

CRITIQUING THE HUMANISTIC PERSPECTIVE

Critics of humanistic psychology have pointed out its strengths and weaknesses. When Rogers began developing his ideas, he was committed to the methods of science and wanted to bring clinical sensitivity, which he saw as lacking in much psychological research, together with scientific rigor. Later in his career, however, he was more interested in the self-reports of clients, emphasizing personal and phenomenological information that he believed provided deeper human insight than typical empirical studies. Hence criticizing the Rogerian view is a bit like trying to hit a moving target.

The intent of the phenomenological approach is to understand human experience as it occurs, appreciating uniquely individual aspects of life as they happen. Thus, the argument goes, the psychologist need not reduce behavior and experience to isolated components, with the resulting loss of personal meaning. However, the critics would say, considering only conscious experience as it is self-reported by individuals inevitably reduces the range of available information; a true science of behavior must include more than phenomenology. And although empathetic observation may well be useful, some might question whether it is reliable and consistent with other approaches to observing and understanding behavior.

Even with these and similar reservations, psychologists today accept the Rogerian notion of self. Research has shown that the self-concept may remain reasonably consistent over time and across different settings—a circumstance that is associated with good psychological health. Some evidence suggests that people of different cultures may construe the idea of self in different ways. Individualistic cultures, for example, often espouse **independent** views whereas collectivist cultures promote **interdependent** views. Such cultural variants may challenge Rogers's conception of self: Individuals in collectivistic cultures are likely to define self-concept in terms of relationships with others, whereas those in an individualistic culture may think of the self as autonomous and unique.

Perhaps the most significant criticism of the humanist perspective is that it has often seemed more philosophical than scientific (and in fact the true existential psychologists have always been vague about the techniques they would recommend). For example, the notion of self-actualization, although an appealing prospect, is more nearly an assumption than a well-demonstrated scientific fact. The definition and measurement of self-based concepts remain somewhat nebulous, at least in part because such measures have typically been self-reports, with all the associated concerns about unreliability and the possibility that individuals will try to "look good." And the assumption that people are naturally good and will make personally fulfilling choices is of course inconsistent with some other philosophical views. Finally, although Rogers espoused a dedication to a scientific approach, he was also willing to sacrifice scientific procedures when he thought they might mean the loss of the richness he perceived in the complexity and phenomenal experience of everyday life.

THE LEGACY OF HUMANISTIC PSYCHOLOGY

Whatever the scientific shortcomings of the humanistic perspective, we must in fairness point out that Rogers and his graduate students did conduct research on the outcomes of therapy, and that Rogers showed (as early as 1954) that his therapy did produce desirable changes. Rogerian ideas have had a prominent position within some areas of the field, especially counseling psychology. Rogers was an advocate for research investigating therapeutic outcomes, a leader in the recording of therapy sessions for evaluative purposes, and the first clinical psychologist to become president of the American Psychological Association after World War II (1946).

Humanistic psychology was particularly popular in the 1960s and 1970s but was never widely embraced by mainstream academic clinical or experimental psychologists. Nevertheless, humanistic psychologists established their own journal (*The Journal of Humanistic Psychology*) in 1961, and a decade later they established the Division of Humanistic Psychology within the American Psychological Association. And Rogers legitimized the idea of research conducted on the effectiveness of psychotherapy. A 1991 survey of psychology department chairpersons found that the chairpersons ranked Rogers the seventh most important psychologist of all time; interestingly, however, historians of the field have not ranked him within the top ten.

Despite existing on the margins of mainstream psychology for much of its life and despite a lack of respect from experimentalists, humanistic psychology has had significant influence on popular culture. The rise of the humanistic perspective came at a time when there was widespread rebellion against authority, and Rogers and his colleagues were also rebelling—against the established authority of psychoanalysis and behaviorism. Indeed, an interesting footnote to this rebellion was a rather famous debate between Rogers and B.F. Skinner in 1956 (Each argued for his own conception of humanity—Skinner his objective, external, scientific view, and Rogers his subjective, internal, humanistic view—and observers concluded that in many ways they were simply arguing at cross purposes). Today, even when his name is not mentioned, we continue to see Rogers's influence in such areas as the protection of the rights of children. Early in his career, Rogers spent 12 years working in the Child Study Department of the Society for the Prevention of Cruelty to Children in Rochester, New York—an experience that he valued quite highly and that influenced his theories about the importance of self-esteem in children. Today we use the terms self, self-concept, self-esteem, self-respect, and self-actualization frequently, even offhandedly. We might do well to reflect on the contributions of the humanistic psychologists to the language we use to try to understand ourselves.

CONCLUSION

The field known as humanistic psychology is an optimistic, positive approach to development of a healthy concept of self. The process of self-actualization is central to the humanistic view of personality in the work of Abraham Maslow and Carl Rogers. Although Maslow believed that most people probably do not achieve self-actualization, he also believed that it is the aim to which psychologically healthy individuals aspire. Self-actualization, however, depends upon prior achievement of lower-level needs.

Each individual develops a self-concept and may compare the reality of the self-concept to an ideal self. If the developing person has not experienced unconditional positive regard, therapy may be helpful in resolving the perceived discrepancy between real and ideal concepts of self. Such therapy, for a Rogerian psychologist, depends upon establishing conditions for unconditional positive regard, empathy, and reflection of a client's phenomenal experience. Although there are scientific limitations inherent in the humanistic approach, it has given us some of the common language of modern psychology and has contributed to the widespread acceptance of the human potential movement.

CHAPTER 6

COGNITIVE PSYCHOLOGY: REVOLUTION OR EVOLUTION?

In the late 19th century, when psychology was emerging as a distinctive discipline and defining itself apart from biology and philosophy, the new experimental psychologists were clearly interested in the mind—consciousness, thought, memory, perception, and other mental processes. Today, these are the subject matters of the field we call **cognitive psychology**. Cognitive psychology concerns itself with the ways we get information, remember and communicate about information, and make decisions or solve problems.

ORIGINS OF COGNITIVE PSYCHOLOGY

Human interest in mental events and processes is not a new thing. As we saw in Chapter 1, scholars have studied language, thinking, perception, and other cognitive topics for 2,000 years or more. When Wilhelm Wundt, the German father of modern psychology, taught his research subjects to use introspection as a tool to understand their perceptions, he was certainly studying cognitive processes. French philosopher René Descartes believed the mind controlled some bodily reflexes, and when Hermann Ebbinghaus used himself as an experimental subject in his studies of memory, he too was engaged in investigations in cognitive psychology.

At the turn of the 20th century, W.H.R. Rivers (1864–1922) was studying the interpretation of visual illusions across cultures, and in 1935 J.R. Stroop (1897–1973) reported the famous effect bearing his name—the tendency for automatic reading responses to interfere with color naming. During and after

The Stroop Effect

In 1935, the *Journal of Experimental Psychology* published an article that was both unlikely and, at the same time, destined to become one of the most famous in the field. J. Ridley Stroop was an unknown graduate student at George Peabody College when he discovered the phenomenon we now call the "Stroop Effect" or the "Stroop Task." Stroop exposed research subjects to color bars and to words denoting color, but printed in different colors (for example, the word "blue" might be printed in red ink). His subjects' task was to name, as quickly as they could, the color of the ink for each item. He found, of course, that people find it difficult to quickly name colors when color words are printed in conflicting colors. He explained this effect by reasoning that we have so much experience with reading that it becomes an automatic, rapid response—in fact, *not* reading the words (instead of naming the color) becomes hard for us. We simply can't help reading the words. On the other hand, recognizing the colors of color bars, without the interference of reading, is easy.

To experience the Stroop Effect, simply say, as quickly as you can, the color (rather than reading the words) of each of the following words:

BLUE	**GREEN**	**YELLOW**
PINK	**RED**	**ORANGE**
GREY	**BLACK**	**PURPLE**
TAN	**WHITE**	**BROWN**

Sources: Galotti, K.M. 1999. *Cognitive Psychology In and Out of the Laboratory*, 2nd ed. Belmont, Calif.: Brooks/Cole-Wadsworth; Goodwin, C.J. 2008. *A History of Modern Psychology*, 3rd ed. New York: John Wiley & Sons.

World War I, German Wolfgang Köhler (1887–1967), working on the island of Tenerife, studied problem solving and insight in chimpanzees, giving a boost to interest in the role of cognition in learning and suggesting that nonhuman animals also engaged in cognitive processes

Edward C. Tolman (1886–1959), working in the 1920s, also studied animals, arguing that rats, for example, could form **cognitive maps** (mental images or representations) of their environment, including important locations and landmarks. Tolman based his conclusions on a series of ingenious experiments in which animals that explored mazes without rewards quickly learned to find the location of goals when rewards were added. These animals, Tolman said, showed **latent learning**—learning that occurs merely through exposure and is not evident at the time when it first occurs.

However, by the time behaviorist John B. Watson (Chapter 2) argued that attempts to study mental activity were not scientific, the field, at least in the United States, had already begun to move away from the study of the mind and toward an objective, rigorous science of observable behavior. The trend away from the study of cognition and mental explanations for behavior continued in the work of prominent behaviorist B.F. Skinner (Chapter 2) who argued that "mental or cognitive explanations are not explanations at all." Explanations for behavior, Skinner believed, lay in the environment, not in the mind. But even during the height of the behavioral era of American psychology in the mid-20th century, cognitive psychologists continued to pursue the study of mental processes. Thus, by 1960 psychologists George Miller and Jerome Bruner had established the Center for Cognitive Studies at Harvard University, and work in the field was especially active in Europe.

Jean Piaget

One example of the European study of cognition can be found in the work of the Swiss psychologist Jean Piaget (1896–1980), which

Jean Piaget *(AFP/Getty)*

Cognition in Rats

Although E.C. Tolman receives credit for his early work investigating cognitive maps in animals, other scientists have also devised clever ways to study cognitive processes in nonhuman species. One such researcher is Richard G. Morris, who developed the **Morris Water Navigation Task** (sometimes called the Morris Maze). The researcher using this task places the rat into a pool of opaque water (see below) containing a submerged escape platform on which the rat can stand. As the rat gains experience swimming in the pool, it is likely to find the platform more quickly—thus providing a measure of the animal's learning and spatial memory.

Source: Morris, R.G.M. 1981. Space localization does not require the presence of local cues. *Learning and Motivation* Vol. 12: 239–260.

Fig 6.1 Morris Water Maze

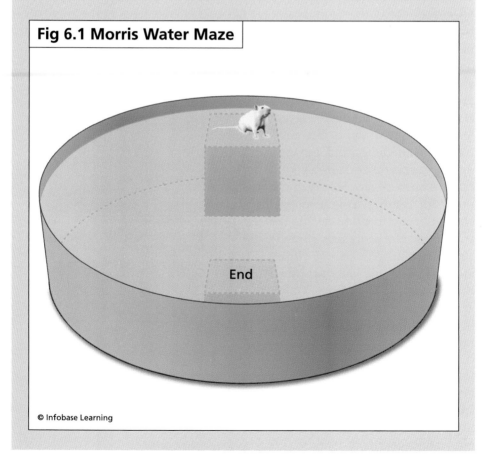

End

began in the 1920s and 1930s and became especially popular because it emphasized the relationship between aging and development of reasoning and conceptual abilities in children. The cognitive abilities of children, Piaget observed, progress through predictable periods characterized by identifiable differences in thought and reasoning. In simplest terms, Piaget identified four major stages of cognitive development:

Sensorimotor Stage—from birth to about 2 years of age, a period during which the child explores the world using the senses and motor activity (touch, taste, vision)

Preoperational Stage—from about 2 to 6 years of age, when the child learns to use language and to understand images but cannot yet think logically

Concrete Operational Stage—from about 7 to 11 years of age, when the child learns to think logically about concrete problems and events but is not yet thinking abstractly

Formal Operational Stage—from about 12 years of age to adulthood, when the child learns to use logical thought to think about abstract concepts and to solve complex problems

Although subsequent research has raised questions about the accuracy of some aspects of Piaget's theory, his work and its widespread acceptance in the middle and late 20th century are representative of the rise of cognitive psychology during this era.

Frederick C. Bartlett

A slightly older contemporary of Piaget was British psychologist Frederick Bartlett (1886–1969). Bartlett gave the field a number of important concepts that underlie memory and cognition, including the notion that we use **schemas** (or **schemata**) to actively organize our experiences. A schema is simply a way of mentally representing or organizing knowledge and experience. These representations, Bartlett thought, help us to reconstruct events that we are trying to remember. Researchers who followed Bartlett came to think of schemata as the basic foundations upon which cognition is built, arguing that this way of mentally organizing experience aided not only memory, but also the learning of concepts, recognition of patterns, and decision making.

Schemata are useful to children as they learn to form and recognize concepts. For example, if a child has a basic framework (schema) for the concept of "kitten," knowing certain fixed characteristics (kittens tend to be small, mammalian, fuzzy, and have tails) may help the child to organize new experiences (e.g., meeting a new kitten) into the existing framework. Schemata can also sometimes serve as **scripts** that guide experiences. If we have a clear idea of what usually happens in a class (students arrive, stop talking when the teacher comes into the room, face the front of the room, and prepare to take notes), this knowledge can become a script that helps us know what to do when we go to a new class or school.

H.M.—Case Study in Memory

The study of memory continued to experience important advances in the middle 20th century. In 1957, William Scoville and Brenda Milner reported the case of a man who had part of his **hippocampus** (a brain structure associated with memory) removed for the purpose of controlling severe epileptic seizures. The man, known as H.M., was 27 years old at the time, and after the operation, seemed unable to transfer information from his short-term memory to long-term memory.

For the rest of his life, H.M. could remember events that had occurred before his surgery but could not create new memories for events happening after the surgery (a condition known as **anterograde amnesia**). He could, however, learn (and remember) new physical (motor) skills, leading researchers to an understanding of the difference between **declarative memory** (memory for knowledge or information, usually verbal, that we think about in a conscious way—like deliberately remembering a list) and **procedural memory** (memory for nonverbal skills or movements that we do not think about in a conscious way—like riding a bicycle).

COGNITIVE PSYCHOLOGY GAINS MOMENTUM

The 1960s brought a period of significant growth of interest in cognitive psychology and its associated areas of research. Some of this interest came from a growing number of psychologists who believed that the behavioral explanations of operant and classical conditioning did not adequately account for such cognitive processes as thinking, memory, and problem solving. However, researchers were also motivated by practical questions (Does observing aggression lead children to behave more aggressively?), by puzzling observations about differences in people (Why are some people optimistic and others pessimistic?), and by technological developments (Can computers think?). Questions like the first led to studies of **social learning** and observational behavior; those like the second resulted in work on **explanatory style**, and questions like the third gave rise to the field of **cognitive science**—an area of interest that overlapped with, but also extended beyond, cognitive psychology.

Social Learning

Social learning theory is associated with the work of Albert Bandura and Julian Rotter. Although both of these researchers have shown a strong interest in behavior, they also believe in the importance of the interaction between how people think and how they act—a **cognitive-behavioral** perspective. It is a concept based on something rather obvious—that people often learn not only through their own direct experience, but also by observing the behavior of others. The study of observational learning has been a hallmark of much of Bandura's work, including classic studies of the effect of aggressive and nonaggressive adult models on aggressive behavior in children (Children observing aggressive adults being rewarded for aggressive behavior behaved more aggressively themselves).

The tendency to learn through observing others is known as **vicarious conditioning**. Bandura has also developed a model to attempt to explain the

Seven: A Magical Number?

In 1956, in one of the most-quoted articles in the history of psychological research, George A. Miller discussed the "magical number seven" in relation to several kinds of cognitive function. He pointed out our fascination with the number seven (the seven seas, seven primary colors, seven notes on the musical scale, seven days of the week, seven ages of man, and so forth), and described several areas of perceptual and cognitive research in which the limits of human performance approximate seven values (as in recognizing auditory pitches and the limits of short-term memory). However, Miller cautioned against reading too much into the fact that several human perceptual and memory abilities shared this apparent limit; it might be, he argued, simply coincidence.

Nevertheless, today most psychology textbooks mention Miller's article and credit him with coining the phrase "magical number seven." And we do know that seven (plus or minus two) meaningful items seems to be the capacity of normal adult **short-term memory.** These meaningful units are known as **chunks**, and may comprise any meaningful grouping of information (often words or numbers). You can demonstrate the effectiveness of chunking by asking a friend to remember the following series of letters: **C   B-S-C   H-E-V   Y-U-S   A-H-B   O-I-P   O-D-U   C-L-A-T   V** . Then repeat the exercise by grouping the letters differently: **CBS   CHEVY   USA   HBO   IPOD   UCLA   TV.** Your friend will be much more likely to remember the letters when you then group them the second way. Meaningless information suddenly becomes a manageable number of meaningful chunks!

Sources: Bernstein, D.A., L.A. Penner, A. Clarke-Stewart, and E.J. Roy. 2008. *Psychology*, 8th ed. Boston: Houghton Mifflin; Miller, G.A. 1956. The Magical Number Seven, Plus or Minus Two: Some Limits on Our Capacity for Processing Information. *Psychological Review*, 63: 81–97.

relations among cognition, behavior, and environment—an interactive model known as **reciprocal determinism**, which is the tendency for each of these entities (cognition, behavior, and environment) to influence and to be influenced by the others. In addition, according to Bandura, a significant aspect of individual cognition is our belief in our own competence, or ability to do things—a characteristic that he calls **self-efficacy**. You may have noticed that your own expectations about your ability to do a task may influence whether you succeed, or even try; when this happens, your own estimate of self-efficacy is at work.

Rotter has taken the cognitive-behavioral perspective in a slightly different direction. His work has examined cognitive aspects of personality and their relation to behavior. The best known part of his theory describes individuals with an **internal locus of control** and those with an **external locus of control**. An internal locus of control implies a belief that the causes of behavior lie within the individual, whereas an external locus of control means that the individual believes the causes are outside the individual. For example, if you should fail an exam and attribute the failure to your own lack of knowledge or intelligence, that illustrates an internal locus of control; on the other hand, if you attribute the failure to bad luck, fate, or an unfair teacher, you are showing a sense of external control. The important issue for Rotter is the *cognitive* interpretation that the person gives to life events.

Explanatory Style

The internal-external locus of control theory bears some similarity to the **explanatory style** concept of contemporary American psychologist Martin Seligman. Seligman has used the concept of explanatory style to account for why some people are persistent and optimistic and why others are pessimistic and give up easily. Explanatory style, according to Seligman, has three dimensions: *permanence*, *pervasiveness*, and *personalization*. Individuals who believe that bad events are likely to last (i.e., are permanent), perhaps affecting them for the rest of their lives, are likely to give up easily in the face of adversity and to be pessimists; in contrast, those who believe good things will last are likely to be more optimistic.

A similar relation exists between pervasiveness (the extent to which something affects a person's entire life) and optimism/pessimism. The person who believes that good things (such as personal intelligence) influence much of life is likely to be optimistic, while one who thinks that bad traits or events ("I'm not good at anything") are pervasive may well become pessimistic. In the same way, the extent to which we personalize events, attributing them to internal or external factors, is also an important part of explanatory style—thus an optimist will attribute good experiences to internal causes (personal characteristics) and bad experiences to external causes (e.g., luck), whereas a pessimist will make the opposite attributions (e.g., good things are due to luck, bad ones to my personal failings). We can see, of course, that the personalization factor, with its internal-external distinction, is similar to Rotter's locus of control theory.

Cognitive Science

By the 1960s, researchers began to consider the likelihood that people are somewhat like computers: For example, they take in data, gather and store information, alter or process information, and make decisions. Computer scientists began studying whether computers could solve problems in the ways that humans do, and whether they might be programmed to use the same kinds of processes that humans use—in short, they were studying **artificial intelligence**, which is the branch of cognitive science that studies efforts to program computers to simulate human intelligence.

The idea of a machine that could engage in human-like cognitive tasks was not entirely new. In the mid-1800s, English mathematician Charles Babbage (1792–1871) envisioned "universal machines" that could perform mathematical calculations; he succeeded in building a small model, but the full-blown version would have been as large as a locomotive and just as expensive. As a result, "Babbage's engines" never became reality. Another Englishman, Alan Turing (1912–1954), approached the same question from a different perspective. Turing, like Babbage, was a mathematician but also served in the British military as a cryptologist. In 1936, Turing wrote a paper in which he tried to show that, hypothetically, a machine could perform any computations, and this became a starting point for development of digital computer programs.

Cognitive science is not, of course, the exclusive domain of computer science; besides cognitive psychology, the field also encompasses aspects of **cultural anthropology**, **linguistics**, and **epistemology** (study of the nature of knowledge). And much work in the field has been interdisciplinary, cutting across two or more of these areas of interest. Recognizing this interconnection, psychologist,

Charles Babbage. *Library of Congress)*

Jerome Bruner observed, ". . . what we needed was an alliance with colleagues from other disciplines who were, each in his or her own context, concerned about how humans acquired and used knowledge." In other words, Bruner had recognized that psychology was too complex to leave to psychologists alone.

COGNITIVE PSYCHOLOGY TODAY

Cognitive psychology has advanced dramatically from the days when serious scientists sometimes criticized cognitive psychologists for their interest in

Cognitive Dissonance

In 1954, social psychologist Leon Festinger (1919–1989) and two colleagues read about a woman (whom they called Mrs. Keech) who claimed to receive messages from superior beings ("Guardians") and who believed that, on December 21 of that year, the Earth would flood, leaving behind only a few chosen people. Festinger had already wondered what would happen when a person strongly believes in something and is then presented with evidence that his or her belief is simply wrong, so he and his colleagues took on assumed names and joined the woman and her group of believers, who were preparing for the future, that is, for life after the impending flood. They were also awaiting instructions from the Guardians, who (group members believed) would send spaceships to rescue the believers. Festinger and his researchers were, of course, observing and making notes on the group's activities.

When December 21 passed with no flood and without the appearance of spaceships, Festinger's group reported what the believers said and did. Interestingly, according to Mrs. Keech, God had saved the world because of the goodness of the group of believers, and the most devout of the believers became more powerfully convinced of the truth of Mrs. Keech's claims, thus reducing the gap between what they believed and the reality of their experience. Examining these responses, Festinger applied them to his original question on what might occur when a strong belief was contradicted by an incompatible reality. According to Festinger, anxiety occurs when we hold incompatible ideas or perceptions in our belief system—a state of affairs he called **cognitive dissonance**. In his view, we tend to reduce the anxiety by altering one of the ideas or by strengthening our justification of the contradiction. Thus, when reality contradicted the beliefs of Mrs. Keech's group, they simply altered their belief and disregarded reality, just as Festinger had predicted!

Sources: Hunt, M. 1994. *The Story of Psychology.* New York: Anchor Books; Matsumoto, D. (Ed.). 2009. *The Cambridge Dictionary of Psychology.* Cambridge, UK: Cambridge University Press.

processes and phenomena that could not be directly observed. Today's cognitive psychologists generally consider themselves experimental psychologists, and they bring the tools of science to bear upon the questions they study. And the questions they study represent a wide range of interests within the field of psychology. As psychology historian C. James Goodwin has noted, cognitive psychology has found its way into research in a variety of subfields, including **social psychology** (with its emphasis on **social cognition**—the influence of information on social behavior and judgment), the relation between brain and behavior, the psychology of personality, and (as we have seen) developmental psychology.

Without question, cognitive psychology and the broader field of cognitive science have become dominant forces on the current scene. In addition to the subfields noted in the previous paragraph, cognitive psychologists may be found studying creativity, intelligence, thinking, sensation, perception, problem solving, and consciousness, to name just a few of their interests. Moreover, we can hardly avoid seeing the products of the work of cognitive psychologists in our everyday environment. They have played a role in the design of many objects and instruments that we regularly encounter: automobile and airplane instrument panels, Websites, computer keyboards, mobile telephones, and educational materials, among many others. In a sense, the growth of cognitive psychology has been a bit like the release of the proverbial genie from the bottle: Its influence has gone well beyond the traditional bounds of psychology and is now a part of a much wider interdisciplinary perspective. Its future will be controlled not only by psychologists, but also by researchers in a variety of related fields, including (at a minimum) computer science, mathematics, linguistics, engineering, and philosophy.

THE LEGACY OF COGNITIVE PSYCHOLOGY

We began this chapter with a question: "Cognitive Psychology: Revolution or Evolution?" The answer is most likely "a bit of both," with the caveat that the latter is more precise than the former. As we have seen, the ideas underlying cognitive psychology are not new. But it was not until mid-20th century that researchers began to truly articulate the defining features of the field we now recognize as cognitive psychology. A pivotal point was the publication (in 1967) of Ulric Neisser's book *Cognitive Psychology*. In this book, Neisser gave the field, in the words of William Shakespeare, "a local habitation and a name." He brought together a range of topics and gave them a common identity, and there followed a rapid growth in the field, leading some observers to call it the "cognitive revolution."

Clearly, there has been a significant increase in scientific work in cognitive psychology in the past few decades, and the cognitive perspective has become an important contributor to research in the field. It continues, however, to have its critics and to grapple with fundamental questions concerning its focus and assumptions. For instance, cognitive psychologists have at times created and discussed "structures" for such processes as memory (e.g., short-term and long-term memory) as if they really existed, thus inviting scientific criticism. B.F. Skinner, for example, pointed out that attributing a phenomenon like memory failure to a hypothetical structure like short-term memory did nothing to further our understanding of the causes of the lapse of memory. If an explanation lies inside the person, the critics have said, we should seek it in such real places as the nervous system—not in invented (or hypothetical) models or structures.

Critics have also questioned the tendency of some cognitive scientists to equate the human mind to computer-like machines. Computers, some skeptics argue, do not experience the powerful influences of emotion, social pressure, and motivation that characterize much of human behavior. Thus, while they may go some distance toward aiding understanding of cognition in its most basic form, computer models fall far short of a thorough *explanation* of complex behavior.

Nevertheless, it is fair to say that cognitive science is found in nearly every corner of today's psychological research world, from the most basic laboratory work to applications in such areas as cognitive-behavioral therapy. Such a proliferation of research and application might lead to the conclusion that we have in fact seen a cognitive revolution. Yet observers of the field are not unanimous in their agreement about this. A scientific revolution, according to physicist Thomas S. Kuhn (1922–1996) occurs when changes in the nature of scientific inquiry produce a rapid transformation of the field (what others came to call **paradigm** shifts).

Did the advent of cognitive psychology sufficiently transform the field of psychology and the nature of its scientific approach to justify calling the changes a revolution? Most historians of psychology seem to conclude that although the rise of the cognitive perspective was a significant change from the preceding behavioral climate, it did not constitute a true revolution in the sense that Kuhn envisioned. Rather, the methods of cognitive researchers embodied much of the scientific approach of behaviorism, gradually adding methods and techniques from the other cognitive sciences. Thus, although it may be too early to assess the true legacy of the cognitive movement, it does seem safe to say we have witnessed not a *revolution*, but instead a cognitive *evolution*.

CONCLUSION

The study of the mind and its associated processes—thinking, perception, memory, and consciousness—was central to the work and interests of the early experimental psychologists who were trying to establish psychology as a distinct science. As the field moved into the 20th century, the possibility of cognition, not only in humans but also in nonhuman species, began to be realized as researchers studied such phenomena as insight and cognitive maps in laboratory animals. At the same time, cognitive psychology gained impetus from the work of scientists interested in the development of cognitive abilities in children and in an understanding of behavior that might go beyond the explanations provided by behaviorism.

In the 20th century the work of computer scientists, linguists, social anthropologists, and others served to expand cognitive science beyond psychology, spurring interest in such areas as artificial intelligence. Within the field of psychology, cognition has found a place in the study of such personal characteristics as locus of control and explanatory style, as well as in social psychology. Although some observers have argued that the cognitive movement brought about a paradigm shift that might be considered a revolution, it seems more prudent (at least at this point in time) to view the development of cognitive psychology as evolutionary.

CHAPTER 7

NEUROSCIENCE AND BIOPSYCHOLOGY: THE FINAL FRONTIER?

"Space," the soothing voice of the *Star Trek* narrator intoned, "the final frontier." Without doubt, the exploration and understanding of space and the secrets of a vast universe represent one end of the spectrum of cutting-edge science. But just as scientists of today believe that the universe extends outward in an infinite array of ever-larger solar systems and galaxies, so too do they believe that it extends in an opposite way, reflected in an increasing understanding of the smallest structures of the universe: cells, molecules, atoms, neutrons, electrons, protons, and quarks. These microscopic and submicroscopic structures are the stuff of human existence, including you and me. And it is within us, particularly in our nervous systems, that many psychological scientists explore their own frontiers, bringing to light a new awareness of the connections between brain and behavior and the role of the nervous system in all of human functioning. In fact, the study of the mind, as physicist and science writer Chet Raymo observed, "will surely be the premier scientific quest of the 21st century." This is the realm of **biological psychology**—a field that some researchers have alternatively called **biopsychology**, **psychobiology**, **behavioral neuroscience**, or **physiological psychology**.

Throughout this chapter, the terms *behavioral neuroscience* and *biopsychology* will be used to represent this field dedicated to understanding the role of biological processes in our everyday behavior and mental processes. It is tempting to assume, perhaps because many biological processes occur unseen within the body or because we have a longstanding tendency to try to separate the physical from the psychological, that biological processes are somehow more fundamental than, or at least different from, psychological processes. However, it is important to recognize that, as psychologist David Myers has observed, "Everything psychological is simultaneously biological." Just as we would not be human without our behavior, thoughts, feelings, and memories, we would also not be human without our brains, nerves, reflexes, or **genes**. Scientists also realize that the interplay between brain and behavior is not only a one-way street—it is a reciprocal relationship in which the brain gives rise to behavior and behavior influences the brain.

THE ROOTS OF BIOPSYCHOLOGY

As we saw in Chapter 1, interest in the biological aspects of psychology began to develop in a serious way in the 19th century. Although some of the early efforts to explain the role of the brain and the nervous system clearly went awry (e.g., phrenology and physiognomy), others, such as the work of Hermann von Helmholtz on conduction of nerve signals, led fairly directly to a more modern view of the connection between nervous system and behavior. And in his 1874 book *Principles of Physiological Psychology,* Wilhelm Wundt hoped to bring together psychology and physiology (some writers in fact suggest that this was the first true psychology textbook). Although the field of biopsychology came out of early work in psychology, more recently the field has relied upon work in many related biological areas, including genetics, physiology, medicine, and evolution.

As the field of psychology evolved, researchers became interested in questions requiring an understanding of the role played by biology. These included questions concerning perception (how we see and hear), the nature and role of hunger and sexual motivation, the character of emotions, why (and how) we sleep, and many others. According to physiological psychologist Neil R. Carlson, although the brain performs many functions, they all boil down to one: controlling movement (behavior). In recent times, this interest in the brain-behavior connection has extended beyond an understanding of the normal activity of the human body to such problems as **schizophrenia** and **depression**, as well as to the link between stress and illness.

NEUROSCIENCE: THE BASICS

The **neuron** (nerve cell) is the basic unit, or building block, of the nervous system, which includes not only the brain and **spinal cord** but also the nerves serving the rest of the body. There as many as 100 billion neurons in the typical human brain (like yours), and like other human cells, each neuron has a cell wall or membrane, a **nucleus** containing genetic material, cytoplasm (fluid), mitochondria (small structures within the cell that produce energy), and other organelles (microscopic structures that aid the functioning of the cell). Neurons consist of three major parts: the **cell body**, also known as the **soma** (soma is the

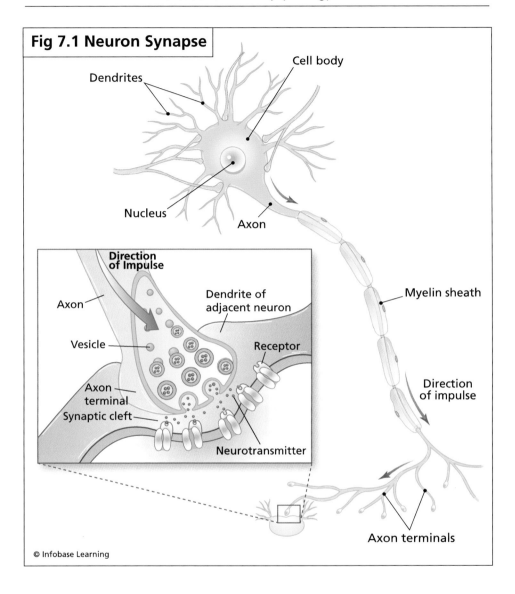

Fig 7.1 Neuron Synapse

Dendrites

Cell body

Nucleus

Axon

Direction of Impulse

Axon

Vesicle

Axon terminal

Synaptic cleft

Dendrite of adjacent neuron

Receptor

Neurotransmitter

Myelin sheath

Direction of impulse

Axon terminals

© Infobase Learning

Greek word for "body"); **dendrites** (branching, bushy fibers extending outward from the cell body); and the **axon** (a long thin fiber that sends messages to other neurons or to muscles and glands). Many axons are covered with a fatty substance known as **myelin**, which protects and speeds nerve signals. Neurons can be extremely small (one millimeter, or about 1/25 of an inch or less in length) or much longer (three feet or more), depending on the length of their axons. A nerve is simply a bundle of axons. It is nerves that connect the body to the brain so that the brain can receive information from the environment and control the body's movement.

Like other cells in the body, neurons contain charged particles called **ions**. When a neuron is at rest, the fluid inside the cell contains a large number of negatively charged potassium ions, and fluid outside the cell has more positively charged sodium ions. When the neuron fires (due to stimulation from the environment or from another neuron), it allows the positive ions to rush in, **depolarizing** the cell (making the inside of the cell more positive) and producing a **refractory** (recovery) **period**, during which the neuron forces the positively charged ions back outside the cell. This process rapidly repeats itself (hundreds of times per second) along the wall of the axon, producing a tiny electrical impulse moving in a direction away from the cell body and toward the **axon terminal**.

Early researchers believed that neurons were attached to one another, but investigators now realize that although neurons may be intertwined, there are microscopic spaces between them—thus producing the **synaptic gap** through which the chemical messengers pass neural impulses from cell to cell. This process—the stimulation of neurons and, in turn, their ability to pass on a message through their influence on other neurons—is the basis for activity not only within the brain, but also in stimulation of muscles and glands and in the relaying of information to and from such sensory organs as the eyes and ears. As the signal travels within a neuron it is electrical; when it reaches the end of the neuron it becomes chemical. Although early scientists assumed that nerve impulses moved at incredibly high speeds, perhaps as fast as the speed of light, we now know that these messages move much more slowly—no more than about 200 miles per hour—due to the chemical portion of the process. And because it involves both electricity and chemistry, we call the process electrochemical.

At the axon terminal, the impulse stimulates the release of chemicals known as **neurotransmitters** from microscopic sacs or **vesicles**. The neurotransmitters flow into the tiny space between the axon terminal and another nerve cell—the synaptic gap—and, if the neurotransmitter molecules reach a site to which they can bind on the receiving neuron, they may stimulate that next cell to fire and the signal may continue on, from neuron to neuron. In some cases, chemicals acting at the synapse may modulate (enhance or weaken) the effects of other neurotransmitters; when this happens, some researchers call these chemicals **neuromodulators**.

THE HUMAN NERVOUS SYSTEM

The nervous system has two major divisions, the **central nervous system** (CNS) and the **peripheral nervous system** (PNS). The CNS is made up of the brain and spinal cord, and the PNS is the network of neurons connecting the CNS to the muscles, glands, and sensory receptors located throughout the rest of the body. Within the PNS, we find two major systems, the **autonomic** (autonomous) **nervous system** and the **somatic** (bodily) **nervous system**.

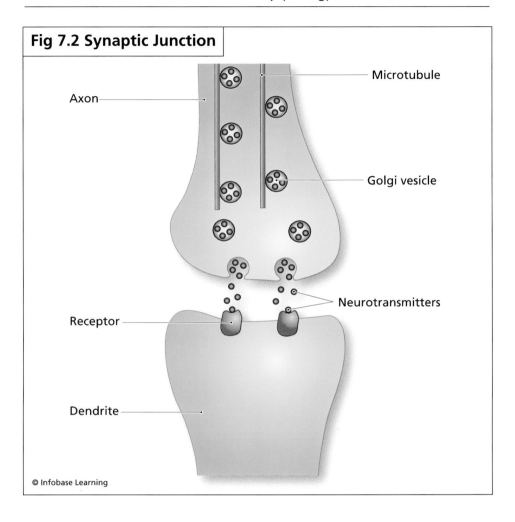

Fig 7.2 Synaptic Junction

Microtubule

Axon

Golgi vesicle

Neurotransmitters

Receptor

Dendrite

© Infobase Learning

Autonomic Nervous System

In simple terms, the autonomic system controls the self-regulating survival functions of the body—such vital organs as the heart and lungs, and various glands—by carrying neural messages to and fro between bodily organs and the CNS. The activities of the autonomic nervous system do not require conscious thought or voluntary action; yet without them we would not survive for long. One branch of the autonomic nervous system, the **sympathetic system**, arouses the body, preparing us for stressful situations by speeding heart rate, stimulating release of adrenalin, slowing digestion, and dilating the pupils of the eyes. If you have ever been very frightened or seriously outraged, you have experienced your sympathetic nervous system at work. The other autonomic branch, the **parasympathetic system**, is instrumental in calming us, slowing heartbeat,

Fig 7.3 Human Nervous System: Detailed Overview

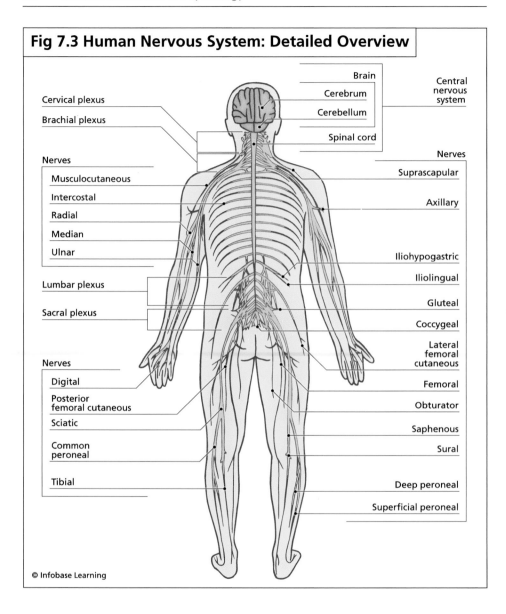

© Infobase Learning

contracting the pupils, and stimulating digestion. Together, these two systems help to keep us on an even keel.

Somatic Nervous System

The somatic nervous system includes the neurons and nerves that communicate signals from the CNS and from the various sense organs of the body. Thus, when you enjoy the sound of music at a concert, or the smell of flowers in a garden, your **sensory neurons**, a part of the somatic nervous system, are at work. Or, when you decide to get up from the kitchen table and move to the television set, your movements are controlled by your **motor neurons**, another part of the somatic nervous system. Because these motor movements are not automatic, psychologists sometimes say the motor neurons control **voluntary behavior**.

The Brain

The human brain is a complex collection of billions of specialized nerve cells located within the skull and combines the electrochemical nature of neuron functions with the biochemistry of these cells to interact with the environment and the rest of the body. If you were to examine a human brain, you would find that it weighs about three pounds, is symmetrical bilaterally (left and right), and is covered with a wrinkled (scientists often say convoluted) surface called the **cortex**. The word cortex comes from the Latin, meaning "bark" (as in the covering of a tree), and it is a thin sheet which, if unfolded and spread out, would be about the size of the front page of a newspaper. The spinal cord extends downward from the brain and is about a foot and a half in length. The spinal cord carries nerves (which in the spinal cord are called **nerve tracts**) in both ascending and descending directions. The right and left halves of the cortex are known as the **cerebral hemispheres**, and are connected to one another by the **corpus callosum**, a large bundle of axons that allows the hemispheres to communicate with each other.

The cortex of the human brain is divided, on each side, into four areas known as **lobes**: the **frontal**, **temporal**, **parietal**, and **occipital** lobes. Although many brain functions occur in several areas of the brain, the four lobes are home to somewhat specialized brain activity. The frontal lobes contain important motor areas, and neurons here have axons extending to cells in the spinal cord, which in turn control muscles. The temporal lobes receive sensory information from the ears, the parietal lobes receive other kinds of sensory information (e.g., from the skin and joints), and the occipital lobes receive and analyze messages from the eyes. The areas of the cortex dealing with information from the senses are known collectively as the **sensory cortex**, and those controlling movement are called the **motor cortex**. Other areas enable thinking, understanding and production of speech and language, and understanding of the world; together, these areas are called the **association cortex**.

The cortex, the uppermost part of the **forebrain**, allows for many of the most advanced human behaviors. However, we would not survive for long without other brain structures. For example, the **hindbrain**, situated at the upper end of the spinal cord, controls a number of functions associated with life maintenance, including heart rate, blood pressure, and breathing. A structure within the hindbrain, the **cerebellum**, plays an important role in coordination,

A House Divided?

We have all heard or read about the presumed specialization of function of the right brain and left brain hemispheres, and popular books exhort us to make better use of our right brain, on the assumption that most of us do not live up to our artistic and spatial potential. Many of us also know of people who, through an accident or stroke, have suffered left brain damage that has impaired their ability to speak. Although the hemispheres constantly communicate, via the 200 million nerve fibers of the corpus callosum, we might wonder how the two sides of the brain would function if their communication were cut off—in other words, if the corpus callosum were severed. Research ethics would of course prevent such surgery for the purpose of scientific curiosity. But in a very small number of patients with extreme, uncontrollable epileptic seizures, surgeons have cut the corpus callosum in a last-ditch attempt to help. This procedure has been successful, and it gives psychologists the opportunity to study the split-brain phenomenon and to draw certain conclusions from such studies.

Research by Roger Sperry and Michael Gazzaniga tested several individuals on whom this surgery had been performed. The tests included evaluation of their visual, tactile (touch), and auditory (hearing) abilities. Sperry and Gazzaniga found that the brain's left hemisphere was superior for speech and that the right hemisphere was better at processing tasks involving shapes and spatial relationships. This does not mean the right hemisphere does not understand language—when asked, for example, to use the left hand (controlled by the right brain) to find objects hidden from view, the subjects could do so, even though they could not name those objects (a left-brain function)! The work of Sperry and Gazzaniga greatly expanded our knowledge of the specialized skills of the two hemispheres of the brain. However, the popular idea that we are more right- or left-brained is a myth that contemporary scientists are continuously working to dispel.

Perhaps the most interesting question about the research described here is this: Aside from their cognitive and spatial abilities, what were these split-brain people really like? Interestingly, they were largely unchanged in personality, emotions, and intelligence; quite understandably, they were also happy to have relief from their seizures. Despite a few occasional oddities (e.g., the left hand returning a book to the desk after the right hand has removed it; or the left brain generating explanations for behaviors initiated by the right brain), these individuals have relatively normal lives.

Source: Hock, R.R. 2002. *Forty Studies That Changed Psychology: Explorations Into the History of Psychological Research*, 4th ed. Upper Saddle River, N.J.: Prentice-Hall.

including the kind of practiced movements we use in playing musical instruments or in dancing, and in some key functions like the timing of our speech. Located above the hindbrain is the **midbrain**, a small brain area that helps us to coordinate sensory input and movement as, for example, when we reflexively look in the direction of a sudden, unexpected noise. Taken together, these structures make up the incredibly complex three-pound organ that is the focus of one of science's most fascinating new frontiers.

THE MODERN NEUROSCIENTISTS

Human beings share some biological characteristics with all other animals, with other vertebrates, other mammals, other primates, and other people. Yet, by virtue of such individual characteristics as our DNA, we are at the same time unique—having some traits that are unlike those of any other person or nonhuman animal. Modern scientists are interested in how the body (including the brain) affects behavior, how behavior affects the body, and how bodily and behavioral functions change together. Instead of accepting the mind-body dualism of 17th-century philosopher and scientist Descartes and his forebears, modern students of biopsychology take an empirical approach to the study of the role of the nervous system in thinking, perception, memory, and behavior.

Examples of the research of these scientists include Charles Scott Sherrington's (1857–1952) explanation of the nature and role of the **synapse**; the work of Karl S. Lashley (1890–1958) on the distribution of memory in the cortex; Roger W. Sperry's (1913–1994) research on split-brain effects, for which he received the 1981 Nobel Prize for Physiology or Medicine; the studies of David Hubel and Torsten Wiesel, who shared the Nobel Prize with Sperry for their work on information processing in the visual system; and the discovery by Patricia Goldman-Rakic (1937–2003) of key aspects of the nature of the frontal cortex and memory. One of the more interesting discoveries in the frontal lobes is the existence of **mirror neurons**, specialized nerve cells that help us to learn by observing others and to understand the feelings of others.

Another Nobel Prize winner, Austrian-born American neuroscientist Eric Kandel, received the 2000 award for his work on the physiological foundations of memory storage, including biochemical changes occurring in neurons in short-term and long-term memory. Following up on the split-brain work of Sperry, Michael S. Gazzaniga has made significant advances in our understanding of the localization of function of the left and right brain hemispheres, and the communication occurring between the hemispheres. And although for many years scientists believed that the structure of the brain was fixed before humans reached adulthood, research psychologist Mark Rosenzweig (1922–2009) and his colleagues found that, even in adulthood, rats living in enriched environments developed a larger cortex. In a similar vein, developmental psychologist

Tiffany Field has shown that touch, in the form of massage, enhances neurological development as well as weight gain in human babies. Further work has discovered, in both humans and nonhuman animals, that repeating a behavior or experience (such as the fingering of notes by stringed instrument musicians) is associated with larger, more complex neural networks in brain areas receiving stimulation from the hand performing the related action.

The examples cited here are just a sample of the amazing number and variety of research areas that psychologists studying brain and behavior are currently pursuing. We have clearly come a long way since the days when Captain FitzRoy's belief in physiognomy nearly kept Charles Darwin off the H.M.S. Beagle, when Paul Broca first became interested in his patient Tan, or when René Descartes dissected the heads of cows in his search for the soul (or mind). The rapid advance in our understanding of biopsychology leads us to wonder what the future may hold in this fascinating area of study.

THE FUTURE OF NEUROSCIENCE

In a recent report on future directions in neuroscience, Steven Rose of England's Open University identified future directions for neuroscience. Below is a small sample of predictions that he and others have made.

Computer Technology

Contemporary neuroscience research is, of necessity, closely linked to advances in technology. And it is in this interface between biopsychology and developing technology that some of our most exciting cutting-edge research takes place. For example, patients are sometimes "locked in" when they experience near total paralysis due to traumatic brain injury, stroke, brain hemorrhage, or damage to neurons caused by such diseases as amyotrophic lateral sclerosis (ALS), commonly known as Lou Gehrig's disease. Recently, researchers have developed technology allowing direct connections between brain and computer, making it possible for such patients to communicate. And beyond communication, recent studies hold the promise of neural interface devices allowing individuals with paralysis to use brain signals to control computers or even robotic devices, and for focused magnetic or electrical stimulation to change brain functions, including mood.

Scanning Technology

Another exciting developing area is the use of imaging techniques to study the living brain. For example, scientists can inject short-lived radioactive chemical tracers (such as radioactive glucose) into the human bloodstream, then follow the metabolism of the chemical using positron emission tomography (PET). Such scans allow researchers to observe which areas of the brain are most active while a person engages in different kinds of cognitive tasks. Another way to

Monkey Think, Monkey Do

Imagine, if you can, that you have had a brain-stem stroke or have ALS (Lou Gehrig's disease), and that you are fully awake and aware of everything around you but cannot move or speak. You are locked in a body that does not function. Then imagine a laboratory monkey, using only its thoughts to control a robotic arm, feeding itself marshmallows. Or a woman, totally paralyzed from the neck down, moving a computer cursor and checking her e-mail, simply by thinking about it. If you think these examples are pure science fiction, think again.

Not only are these cases real, but a research team at Duke University, led by scientist Miguel Nicolelis, has succeeded in teaching a monkey working in their lab in the United States to control a robot walking in a Japanese lab, by using only its thoughts. These projects rely on a technology known as Brain-Machine Interface (BMI) that involves recording neural activity via electrodes implanted in the cortex and then using the input to control electronic or electromechanical devices. At present, this work remains in an experimental phase, but researchers have conducted several trials with humans and have demonstrated the feasibility of the technology for practical use (e.g., monkeys feeding themselves). Although the current technology is too cumbersome for practical use, it seems clear that these "neuroprosthetic controllers" are a beacon of hope for locked-in patients.

Source: Patoine, B. Brain-Machine Interfaces: Sci-fi Concepts Make Clinical Inroads. In B. Mauk (Ed.), *2009 Progress Report on Brain Research*. New York: The Dana Alliance for Brain Initiatives. 43–52.

create detailed maps of brain activity uses functional magnetic resonance imaging (fMRI)—a technology depending on rapid oscillation of magnetic fields to discover small changes in metabolism in active areas of the brain. An even more direct measure of brain activity is **magnetoencephalography** (MEG), a technology based upon monitoring of tiny magnetic fields associated with the electrical activity of the brain. Although MEG measurements can be more precise than fMRIs, their visual resolution is not as good—leading researchers to work toward combining these technologies. These and other similar technological advances allow researchers to literally "picture" the living brain at work.

Psychopharmaceuticals and Pharmacogenetics

The World Health Organization has described depression as a major epidemic, predicting that, by the year 2020, it will be the world's second most devastating illness (after heart disease). Researchers have made advances in development of treatments for depression, including medications. But as more and more people use these drugs, so too do more people experience dangerous side effects. In addition, different people respond differently to various drugs, and drugs that some use safely can cause bad reactions in others. Researchers are asking

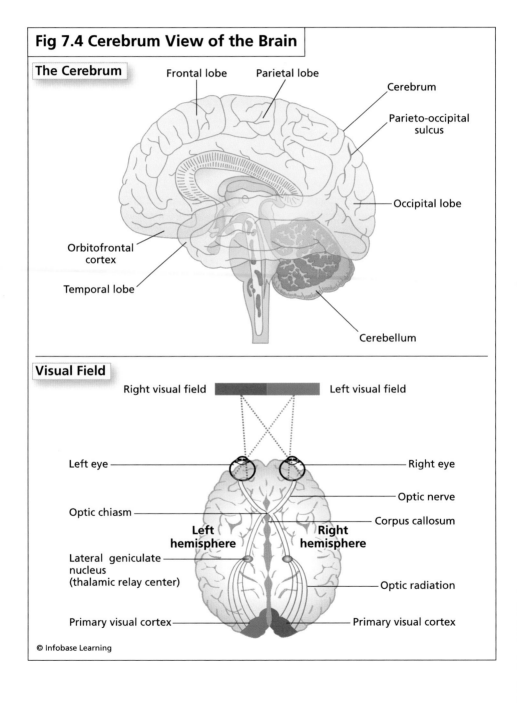

Fig 7.4 Cerebrum View of the Brain

The Cerebrum

Frontal lobe   Parietal lobe

Cerebrum

Parieto-occipital sulcus

Occipital lobe

Orbitofrontal cortex

Temporal lobe

Cerebellum

Visual Field

Right visual field   Left visual field

Left eye   Right eye

Optic nerve

Optic chiasm

Corpus callosum

Left hemisphere   **Right hemisphere**

Lateral geniculate nucleus (thalamic relay center)

Optic radiation

Primary visual cortex   Primary visual cortex

© Infobase Learning

whether some of the differential effects engendered by medications could be due to genetic differences in the people taking them. Thus, scientists are interested in learning whether genetic tests can be developed to identify genetic markers that would allow identification, in advance, of people who would benefit from (or be harmed by) various drugs. Developments in this area of research could potentially improve the lives of millions of people with depression, schizophrenia, and other serious disorders.

The Aging Brain

In the industrialized countries of the world, the average life span has steadily increased. A few hundred years ago, in the Medieval period, life expectancy at birth was between 30 and 35 years; now the world average is in the mid to upper 60s, and in some countries (e.g., Japan) it is around 80. As the population ages, we become increasingly aware of the loss of cognitive function that sometimes accompanies aging. So, as people get older, they are more likely to experience not only the normal declines associated with age, but also to have such neurodegenerative conditions as Alzheimer's disease. Neuroscientists will continue to work to develop improved understanding of the biochemical and genetic aspects of the processes that lead to Alzheimer's, the improvement of medications that slow its progression, and possible new immunological techniques aimed at preventing the brain deterioration associated with the disease.

Although space, as the *Star Trek* narrator observed, is surely a wondrous scientific frontier, it is hard to imagine research challenges more fascinating, complex, and important than those facing the scientists who study the brain and its connections to everyday human behavior. Writer and Parkinson's disease patient Joel Havemann summed this up in a manner both apt and eloquent:

> What seems astonishing is that a mere three-pound object, made of the same atoms that constitute everything else under the sun, is capable of directing virtually everything that humans have done: flying to the moon and hitting seventy home runs, writing Hamlet and building the Taj Mahal—even unlocking the secrets of the brain itself.

CONCLUSION

The study of the connection between brain and behavior, between the nervous system and all of human functioning, is the realm of biopsychology, or behavioral neuroscience. It is a field populated not only by psychologists but by other scientists as well, such as those specializing in such areas as genetics, physiology, medicine, and evolution. Neuroscientists have illuminated the structure and functions of the nervous system, from the electrochemistry of the neuron to technologically sophisticated scans of the brain, expanding our basic scientific knowledge and our ability to apply this knowledge to human problems.

As biopsychological knowledge continues to grow, neuroscientists see more exciting developments on the horizon. The potential exists for treatment of some of our most vexing brain-based diseases—such as Alzheimer's disease and Parkinson's disease—and for answers to the centuries-old questions, raised by every civilization since the ancient Greeks, about the nature of the mind. Exploration of inner space is proving every bit as intriguing as that of outer space.

CHAPTER 8

A PSYCHOLOGY OF ALL PEOPLE: THE SOCIOCULTURAL APPROACH

According to an old Asian proverb, a frog in a well cannot comprehend the ocean. In some versions of the story, the frog assumes that the sun and the moon shining down upon his little well shine only for him, and that his well is, for all practical purposes, the universe. The frog does not, in fact, realize that he lives in a well. For too much of its history, the psychology we have studied in America has resembled the frog in the well. Our little corner of the field was a perfectly fine universe, and there was little need to think about the world beyond its boundaries. For psychology, as we have often taught it in the United States, has been largely North American psychology, based on research conducted largely by North Americans and using largely North Americans as research subjects. However, this situation has begun to change, and that is the story of a **sociocultural approach** to psychology. In short, psychologists interested in the sociocultural approach see social and cultural background as important contributors to human behavior and psychological characteristics.

As recently as the 1960s and 1970s, general psychology textbooks contained few references to **culture** and its role in influencing psychological phenomena. When such books did mention culture, it was usually a brief acknowledgement of cultural anthropologists, such as Margaret Mead (1901–1978), or a discussion of possible IQ differences between black Americans and white Americans. There was little indication of the likelihood that culture, and the experience of people within their own unique cultures, might influence such fundamental psychological processes as development, learning, perception, social behavior, or abnormal behavior. And students were learning a psychology that was essentially white, as African American psychologist Robert Guthrie (1930–2005) suggested in the title of his book on the subject, *Even the Rat Was White*. Although we still have plenty of room for growth in our understanding of the relation between culture and psychology, we have come a long way in the past few years.

CULTURE: WHAT IS IT?

Culture has been the subject of study and description by many investigators, including not only psychologists, but also sociologists, anthropologists, and others. Some of these researchers have defined culture in terms of groups of people who share a particular place and a common set of experiences or language. Others have applied the label *culture* to religions, socioeconomic groups, and regions within a country, or simply a way of life shared by a group. Researchers have identified characteristics of culture that they consider "objective," including the tangible objects produced by the group: food, furniture, buildings, or works of art. And they have called other aspects of culture "subjective": political processes, religion, and social practices, among others.

One useful step in defining culture is identification of those human characteristics that do *not*, at least when considered in isolation, constitute culture. Foremost among these are nationality and race. Imagine that someone asks you to define American culture. Will you describe Little Italy in New York City? Koreatown in Los Angeles? the farm country of Iowa? the mining culture of West Virginia? It is easy to see that in a nation as diverse as the United States, it does not make much sense to talk about *the* culture. Some nations are homogeneous, with a clearly dominant national culture, but many others (including the United States) are too diverse to classify in such a simple way. Similarly, race alone cannot define culture. Not only is race not nearly as clearly biologically defined as many people seem to believe, but people of similar racial background may also have vastly different cultural experiences and characteristics. Black people of African descent currently living in the United States, for example, may live very different lives from others, also of African descent, who live in other countries. Psychologists who study different cultural groups that encounter one another in the same broader cultural context (e.g., within the same nation) are known as **multicultural psychologists**; those who study people living in different nations or cultures are **cross-cultural psychologists**.

So what then is culture? Most researchers who have attempted to define culture have included two essential ingredients: First, culture involves *a set of behaviors, values, and beliefs* shared by members of a group; second, *members of the group pass these behaviors, values, and beliefs from one generation to the next.* The first part of this definition identifies the characteristics that people of a social *group* are likely to hold in common. The second part of the definition sets cultural characteristics apart from individual characteristics like personality—

which may also involve behaviors, values, and beliefs, but which are associated with the life of *one* person.

CULTURE AND PSYCHOLOGY: HISTORICAL ROOTS

Like many subjects that psychologists study, sociocultural interests may seem, on the one hand, to be of recent origin. But on the other hand, they have probably existed as long as there have been humans around to think about them. As early as several centuries B.C.E., for example, Herodutus had a low opinion of people who did not speak Greek, while Hecataeus of Miletus was calling Greek traditions "ridiculous."

In more recent times, English anthropologist and psychiatrist W.H.R. Rivers (1864–1922) was interested in vision and perception of cultural groups. Near the turn of the 20th century, Rivers accompanied a British expedition to the Torres Straits (between Australia and New Guinea), where he studied color vision and the effects of perceptual illusions on islanders there. Rivers described similarities and differences between the islanders and the people of England and India, thereby becoming one of the earliest scientists to consider the influence of culture on basic psychological processes.

Writing at about the same time as Rivers, American scholar W.G. Sumner (1840–1910), in reporting characteristics of various cultures, became the first person to use the word **ethnocentrism**—the tendency of people to view their own culture as superior to others. In retrospect, some of Sumner's examples are amusing; he described, for example, how Tupi people (native to Brazil) ridiculed the Portuguese by calling them a derisive name meaning birds with feathered feet (because they wore trousers!). Nevertheless, Sumner, like Rivers, was beginning to appreciate the connection between culture and behavior. And Wilhelm Wundt, best known as the father of experimental psychology (Chapter 1), also studied the influence of culture on individuals, eventually publishing a multivolume series on folk psychology. So we can see examples of a longstanding interest in culture and psychology, although until recently much of the field badly neglected the subject.

CULTURE AND PSYCHOLOGY TODAY

A quick review of several popular modern introductory psychology textbooks shows a much broader coverage of culture than books of three or four decades ago. Today, culture appears in sections dealing with abnormality, achievement motivation, aggression, alcohol, altered states of consciousness, archetypes, attachment, attitudes, attractiveness, attribution, cognitive development, communication, and so on, right up to psychotherapy, relationships, self-esteem, sexual behavior, sleep, socialization, teaching styles, testing, temperament, and more. It seems clear that we have come a long way toward integrating the sociocultural perspective into mainstream psychology.

The Carpentered World

Consider the figure below. You have no doubt seen this figure before, and you perhaps know that line (a) and line (b) are the same length, although line (b) appears longer. What you may not have considered, is that your perception of this illusion (the **Müller-Lyer Illusion**) may depend, at least in part, on your cultural experience. When W.H.R. Rivers studied perceptions of Torres Straits islanders more than a century ago, he expected these less "civilized" people to make more errors in judging the lengths of the lines than did English people. To his surprise, the islanders' judgments were more accurate. Why might this be?

Although researchers have proposed several possible explanations for these findings, one interesting possibility is that people of Western cultures live in "boxes." If we live in a Western culture, we spend our days living in, viewing, and passing through, square city blocks, rectangular rooms, perpendicular walls, and rectangular doors. We learn skills and perceptual expectations about judging distances and lengths based upon the angles and line lengths in our everyday boxes. If you are sitting in a room as you read this, look at the nearest corner. You will find that the line formed by the perpendicular walls intersects the floor and ceiling in the same way the short lines intersect the long lines of the Müller-Lyer figure. People who have not lived in rectangular structures develop different ways of perceiving their environment, and they do not have the same experience judging length and distance based upon those structures. Hence the **carpentered world hypothesis** is an attempt to explain the cultural difference.

8.1 Müller-Lyer Figure

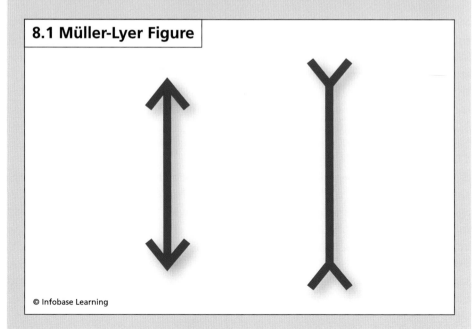

© Infobase Learning

If our sociocultural backdrop influences all the psychological issues and processes noted in the previous paragraph, we might reasonably ask whether there are any unifying or overarching principles that could help us to see the big picture. At least five fundamental conclusions seem warranted.

Culture is a Psychological Construct

Although it is true that culture comprises both objective and subjective characteristics, most writers in the field nevertheless seem to consider culture primarily subjective. Accordingly, although such features as architecture or food may be important in understanding a region or a culture, they do not define culture as clearly as the human characteristics of members of the group: their behaviors, attitudes, values, and beliefs. To put this another way, we might agree that much of what defines sociocultural influence is not those things we can *see*, but rather those things we *infer* about people. If we are interested in attitudes or values, for example, we may not actually be able to see those characteristics; instead, we infer them, either from observable behavior of people or from objective products of the group (e.g., the building of churches or schools).

Even such observable personal characteristics as race seem, in fact, to be psychological constructs. Genetic research, for example, has indicated that biological differences between people of various races are actually comparatively superficial, resulting in the conclusion that race is largely a psychosocially constructed notion (some researchers have gone so far as to call it an illusion). In many ways, John Locke had it right when he characterized the child as a blank page upon which experience writes—and that experience is largely sociocultural, as it plays out in the practices of parents, schools, religions, communities, and all the other aspects of cultural structure.

People Are More Alike Than Different

If you visit another country, another region, or perhaps even another family in your own city, you may find striking the obvious differences between the "other" and yourself. These people may eat different foods, speak different languages, believe in different things, treat family members differently, use different forms of transportation, or behave differently toward outsiders. You may be tempted to conclude they are very different from you. For many years, those psychologists who did show an interest in culture focused mostly on describing such differences, leading to the conclusion that members of different groups were psychologically very different from one another.

More recently, however, researchers have developed more sophisticated ways of thinking about differences across groups of people. Among the things this new research has shown is that it is possible for measured differences in psychological characteristics (e.g., motivation, personality, or intelligence) to be **statistically significant**, but not of practical significance. For example, in research using very large samples an average difference as small as one point on an IQ test might well be statistically significant; on the other hand, if the samples are very small, an IQ difference as large as 15 or 20 points might not prove statistically significant, depending upon such factors as the variability of the scores and the statistical techniques scientists use to compare them. Although the very small difference between large groups may be reliable, and thus statistically significant, we would probably not argue that a difference of a single point (on a scale of more than 150) is of any real importance. At the present time, scientists are not only using better statistical procedures to evaluate differences between groups, but are also counseling against the use of small group differences to make general inferences about groups; in other words, we must be careful to avoid **stereotyping** groups based upon small statistical differences. Instead, we need to be aware that all social and cultural groups face similar goals and problems (e.g., reproducing and raising families, dealing with threats to health and safety) and that individuals within groups may well be different from the majority or even the average for their group.

We See Others from Our Own Perspective

When we encounter others whom we perceive to be different from us, we are likely to have some predictable reactions. It seems to be human nature, for instance, to use our own cultural experience as a standard and to judge a different group in that light—usually concluding that our own experience is superior. We may also become suspicious of unfamiliar others, develop stereotyped views of them, and even come into conflict with them. This universal tendency is what W.G. Sumner, writing more than a century ago, called *ethnocentrism*. Even earlier, Charles Darwin observed the tendency of tribes to be more sympathetic toward their own groups than toward others. Researchers have found that people tend to be ethnocentric toward ethnic minority groups, across nationalities, and toward people with disabilities. And researchers themselves are not exempt from ethnocentric tendencies; contemporary authors have noted that the writings of early psychologists of the stature of G. Stanley Hall and Francis Galton reveal that they were ethnocentric.

Studies show that people who are especially likely to be ethnocentric include those who are self-centered, religious fundamentalists, intolerant of ambiguity, and authoritarian. Levels of ethnocentrism also seem to vary across cultural groups. Investigators have studied various ways to attempt to overcome ethnocentrism; they have found that education may play a role in reducing ethnocentrism and that contact with specific groups of "others" has sometimes helped. However, contact alone, without social support and equal status between the groups, does not always reduce ethnocentrism. At its extreme, ethnocentric bias emerged in the work of such writers as French philosopher Lucien Lévy-Bruhl (1857–1939), who supported the notion of a binary "Great Divide" theory, viewing cultures as either Western or "primitive." Today's researchers have a much more enlightened view of people and of the world, but the fact remains that most people continue to experience ethnocentrism in their encounters with those who are different from themselves.

Cultural Groups Differ Along Psychological Dimensions

Groups and individuals vary in the extent to which they look to long-term rewards in lieu of short-term gains (**long-term orientation**); attempt to reduce or avoid ambiguity and uncertainty (**uncertainty avoidance**); expect or accept inequality between group members (**power distance**); show traditional gender roles and distinctions (**masculinity-femininity**); and pursue individual goals that are similar to, or different from, those of the group (**individualism-collectivism**). Of these dimensions, the best known and most thoroughly researched is individualism-collectivism.

Individualism-collectivism has been subject of many investigations, and the terms "individualist" and "collectivist" have found their way into our everyday language. It has become common, both in writing and in conversation, for people to refer to others who are self-centered or ambitious as individualists, and to characterize entire nations (e.g., Japan) as collectivist. Unfortunately, this kind of labeling is at best an oversimplification and at worst a dangerous exercise in stereotyping. Recent research includes numerous studies revealing many individualists living in so-called collectivist nations, just as many collectivists live in nations (like the United States) presumed to be individualistic. The message in this, according to scientists who study sociocultural variables, is that we must look to *individuals*, not generalizations, to fully appreciate the role of cultural influence.

Some Psychological Truths Are Universal, Some Not

Sometimes our textbooks present psychological principles as if they are universal truths, with no allowance for the possible influence of culture. However, just as the force of gravity varies with size and distance, psychological truths may vary with individual social and cultural experience. One person's hallucination may be another person's vision; one person's eye contact may be another person's angry stare. The sociocultural approach requires that we try to determine whether our knowledge is true for all people in all circumstances, or if it is limited to some groups—nationalities, ethnic groups, people of certain sexual orientation or gender, etc.

This interest in determining the nature of psychological truth has led to development of special nomenclature. We use the term **etic** to refer to those psychological principles that seem to be universal, and those that seem to be culture-limited or culture-bound are known as **emics**. These terms have their roots in the study of linguistics, with *etic* coming from the word "phonetic" (using the International Phonetic Alphabet, it is possible to form the sounds of any spoken language), and *emic* coming from "phonemic" (each language has its own unique set of basic sounds—its phonemes). In American schools, for example, the importance of teaching children independent thinking might be an emic (important to the particular culture, but perhaps not to all cultures); similarly, there are probably etic aspects of the notion of intelligence (e.g., ability to solve problems) that are important to all cultures (although the tools they use to solve problems may vary widely from culture to culture).

EXAMPLES OF SOCIOCULTURAL INFLUENCE

Scientists have found examples of sociocultural influence in nearly all subfields of psychology. Here we will review just a few examples from mainstream areas of psychology—development, personality, abnormal psychology, social psychology, and memory—as a way of illustrating the importance of sociocultural understanding.

Developmental Psychology

As explained in Chapter 6, the work of Jean Piaget has been important in psychology's conceptualization of the way children develop cognitive abilities. For many years, Piaget's work went largely unquestioned—we assumed that cognitive development proceeded more or less as he had described it. But a sociocultural approach argues that cognitive development must be understood in its cultural context. We now know that tasks within Piaget's stages may occur in different orders across cultures, even though the stages themselves seem to occur in the same order. And, when people in some cultures, or with some kinds of experience within a particular culture, do not achieve Piaget's stage of formal operations, we should understand that this stage is associated with formal Western-style education. Cultures (or individuals) that do not achieve this stage are not "primitive" or "unintelligent" but may simply not consider scientific reasoning the ultimate goal of cognitive development.

Cultures and subcultural groups also differ in how they perceive aging, an aspect of lifespan development that researchers have studied by analyzing the portrayal of elderly individuals in advertising. In the United States, for example, studies have shown that elderly people are often the focus of health-related advertisements, and often appear in such ads along with other older people. In contrast, older people featured in advertisements in India are more likely to appear in ads for financial services, often surrounded by members of extended families. Investigators have attributed these differences in the depiction of the elderly to very different sociocultural attitudes about aging and the elderly. The U.S. perception is more indicative of negative stereotypes and segregated lifestyles; the Indian perception shows something akin to reverence and inclusion.

Views of Personality

A persistent question in psychology has been why people are the way they are—how we arrive at our views of self and the characteristics that define each of us. Western psychology has concerned itself mainly with European and American approaches to understanding personality, less often addressing Eastern viewpoints. Typical Western perspectives assume that humans are individual, autonomous agents, defining themselves independently of others. Thus, the independent ego is likely to be an important aspect of personality development, and the view of self is predicated on unique personal characteristics and individual aspirations, a concept psychologists call **independent self-construal**. The Western self can coexist within groups but does so mostly as an independent entity because individualism inhibits overlapping with others. The self has clear boundaries and is unique to the individual.

Eastern views of personality, particularly those arising from Buddhist or Confucian backdrops, place a high value on the role of group membership (especially in families) as an influence on personality. They are more likely to be other-centered and to define the concept of self as an entity overlapping with the self views of others in important groups (family, friends, co-workers, etc.). The independent ego is problematic, because it is associated with loneliness, greed, pride, and other non-engaged emotions. Researchers sometimes label the Eastern notion of self as **interdependent self-construal**, implying that we can define individual personality only in relation to others.

What Is Abnormal?

Some psychological disorders, including schizophrenia and depression, seem to occur universally across cultures and subcultural groups. Yet even these universal problems occur differently in different sociocultural contexts, and the circumstances under which people recover from them also may vary from one setting to another. Schizophrenia, for example, may include both **positive symptoms** and **negative symptoms**. Positive symptoms are excessive or distorted behaviors like delusions, hallucinations, or disorganized speech. Negative symptoms are reduced or omitted behaviors, such as diminished speech, lack of emotion, or withdrawal. Although schizophrenia is universal, sociocultural factors appear to influence *how* people express their symptoms; hence, Americans are more likely than Japanese people to express positive symptoms, and the Japanese are more likely to experience passive, withdrawn negative symptoms.

Within the United States, cultural and ethnic differences, coupled with socioeconomic factors, are associated with a number of interesting variations in the occurrence of psychological disorders. Studies have shown that African Americans may experience higher rates of bipolar disorder and schizophrenia than European Americans but a lower incidence of panic disorder and

Is Mental Health a Sociocultural Construct?

Although psychologists consider some disorders to be universal across both cultures and subcultures, there is a fascinating array of mental health problems that are unique to particular cultures or contexts. Consider, for example, being a student in West Africa. As exam time approaches, you might experience *brain fag*—headaches, lack of concentration, and eye fatigue. Or, imagine yourself as a Japanese "salaryman." Working extremely long hours under great work-related stress, you might be vulnerable to *karoshi*, or "death from overwork." According to some estimates, *karoshi* is a condition that (by the 1990s) had killed as many as 10,000 people per year (through heart and brain diseases). If you lived above the Arctic Circle, in isolation and lacking sufficient calcium in your diet, you might be moved to throw off your clothes and rush out into the brutal Arctic winter—a condition known as *pibloktoq*. And you don't even need to leave Western society to see sociocultural mental health constructs. Take for example the common phrase "running amok" that Westerners generally use to describe someone behaving in a manner that is wildly out of control. The phrase comes from *amok*, a Southeast Asian disorder that causes people (most often male) to engage in sudden violent, wild aggression toward another person.

Occasionally, a behavior that many people might see as abnormal becomes more or less acceptable in its sociocultural context. This is the case with "fear of going home syndrome" in Japan—seen in Japanese salarymen who, instead of going home after work, may choose to spend extensive time with coworkers. Although outsiders might consider this behavior abnormal, some people in Japan would not label it a disorder, but would instead consider it normal (This true fear of going home is different from the Western worker who might simply "hang out" with friends or co-workers before going home late). It seems clear that the definition of abnormal behavior bears a definite relation to the sociocultural context in which it occurs.

Sources: Berry, J.W., Y.H. Poortinga, M.H. Segall, and P.R. Dasen. 2002. *Cross-Cultural Psychology: Research and Applications*, 2nd ed. Cambridge, UK: Cambridge University Press; Lafayette De Mente, B. 2002. Asian Business Codewords. *Asia Pacific Management Forum*, May 2002, available at http://www.apmforum.com/columns/boye51.htm.

depression. Although some research has indicated that Asian Americans experience higher levels of disorders than European Americans, and Latino Americans about the same as European Americans, more detailed analysis shows fairly widespread differences within each of these groups. Chinese Americans, Vietnamese Americans, Japanese Americans, and Korean Americans (as well as a number of others of Asian origin) differ from each other just as surely as do Mexican Americans, Puerto Ricans, Cuban Americans, and other Latinos. Clearly, sociocultural experience and context are relevant to an understanding of the concept of abnormal behavior.

Social Behavior

When people act in a particular way in social situations, they have a natural tendency to draw conclusions about the causes of their behavior. Social psychologists have conducted numerous investigations of this inclination to make assumptions about why people behave in the ways they do, and they have given it a name: **attribution**. Imagine that you are a worker and that you frequently arrive late for work. What will your employer think about your behavior? Will he or she assume that you are lazy, irresponsible, or uncaring? Or will the employer assume you had an unavoidable problem with your car, that your train arrived late, or that you are ill? The first list of possible causes for your behavior are **dispositional** (psychological traits or characteristics of the person), and the second list comprises possible causes that are **situational** (associated with the environment or the situation). How we make attributions for behavior, whether our own or that of someone else, bears an interesting relation to culture and experience.

Some people (individualists) are likely to make dispositional attributions about the failings of others; if you are late for work, the boss may therefore be quick to assume you are just lazy. Individualists are likely to see events as less dependent on context (situation) and more independent on person (disposition). So the boss sees *you* as responsible for your tardiness. Collectivists, on the other hand, are more likely to see behavior in its situational context and to assume that the context shapes personal behavior; in this case, the boss might be quick to assume that some *situational* problem (like a late train) caused you to be tardy. Interestingly, when we are judging our own behavior, we may make attributions that are different from those we assign to the behavior of other people: If I am an individualist and arrive late for work, I may blame my faulty alarm clock or traffic on the freeway; if I'm a collectivist, I'm likely to blame myself, and say I must learn to be more responsible. Social psychologists Carol Tavris and Elliot Aronson have discussed a number of aspects of belief, blame, decision making, and other elements of social behavior in their book *Mistakes Were Made (But Not by Me)*.

Memory

At first glance, you might be tempted to conclude that memory would not be subject to sociocultural forces—or at least that it would be less so than other psychological processes. After all, you may say, we each have a good memory or a poor memory. However, like many apparently simple scientific conclusions, this one is incorrect, or at least incomplete. In fact, people of different cultural backgrounds show interesting differences in memory skills, and these differences seem to be associated with their respective sociocultural experience. One memory phenomenon described in many psychology textbooks is the **serial position effect**—the tendency, when we have memorized a list, to better remember items near the beginning or the end of the list while forgetting items in the middle of the list. Although the serial position effect may be familiar to any educated person who has forgotten items from a shopping list, research has suggested that people without formal schooling do not experience this effect—a result occurring across cultural groups.

The serial position effect is probably a product of the kind of educational experience that encourages writing (as in note taking) and list making as aids to retention of important information. These techniques are not, of course, common to all cultural and subcultural groups. Other cultural and ethnic groups have different customs and traditions associated with memory. Individuals from groups with a strong oral tradition, and a custom of storytelling, remember stories more reliably than people educated in formal Western schools. Despite

Can't Remember Your Grocery List?

Try this exercise and experience the serial position effect for yourself:

1. Give yourself 60 seconds to memorize the following list of words.
2. Cover the list and write the words, in order.
3. Check your list against the original list.

mirror	wheel
book	letter
garden	window
pillow	person
library	

If you are a typical product of the American educational system, you probably remembered more of the words near the beginning and end of the list, and you probably forgot more from the middle of the list. The tendency to remember words early in the list is the **primacy effect**; the tendency to remember those near the end is the **recency effect**.

these and other cultural differences in memory, at least one finding seems to be universal: As people age, their memory-related abilities tend to decline. Like other areas of psychological study, human memory shows both universal and culture-limited characteristics.

THE FUTURE OF THE SOCIOCULTURAL APPROACH
Many contemporary scientists conduct sociocultural research in areas like cross-cultural psychology, multicultural psychology, social identity, acculturation, biculturalism, and ethnicity. Interest in these areas has increased in the past few decades, with many university courses addressing cultural issues, and a growing body of knowledge about the connection between culture and the body of psychological science. The increasing emphasis on sociocultural influences is likely to continue for the foreseeable future, as America grapples with such social issues as immigration, diversity, discrimination, and international conflict. However, some cultural psychologists anticipate a longer-term future in which sociocultural variables will be integrated with teaching and research in mainstream psychology. If that day eventually arrives, perhaps the sociocultural approach will have achieved its aims, making a separate focus on culture no longer necessary.

CONCLUSION
The sociocultural approach to psychology is concerned with understanding the role of social and cultural contributions to human behavior and psychological characteristics. Although much of North American psychology has been based on research findings gathered from people with somewhat homogeneous culture and ethnicity, the field has changed in recent years to accommodate increasing inclusion and consideration of sociocultural influences. Psychologists have defined culture as a set of common behaviors, values, and beliefs that members of the group pass on from generation to generation. Although we often think of cultures in terms of nations, it is also the case that many nations are quite culturally diverse, encompassing diverse subcultures.

Some psychological principles (etics) are universally valid, and others (emics) are limited to specific cultural or subcultural groups. Recognition of this distinction has led to a significant body of research showing that many mainstream psychological findings are not universal, as psychologists may previously have believed. Instead, sociocultural experience and context are significant influences that scientists must take into account when drawing conclusions about the nature and effects of psychological principles. Although the subfields of psychology that specialize in cultural effects continue to grow, many cultural psychologists hope that the field will eventually integrate sociocultural issues, making a specialized focus on culture unnecessary.

CHAPTER 9

PSYCHOLOGY GOES TO WORK: APPLICATIONS AND CAREERS

In Chapter 1, we met E.B. Titchener, the early experimental psychologist who, following his doctoral studies with Wilhelm Wundt in Germany, moved to America to pursue his work with structuralism. Unlike his colleagues in the functionalist movement, Titchener had no interest in applied psychology. But while structuralism was dying on the vine, new uses for the budding field of psychology were about to blossom. In this chapter we will review the movement of psychology from the experimental laboratory into applications in a variety of settings.

In Chapter 4 we discussed the development of group testing in the World War I era as a response to the practical need for assessing large numbers of military personnel; a decade or two earlier, prominent psychologist G. Stanley Hall had established the child study movement. The aim of the child study movement was to conduct extensive research on children as a means to a greater end—findings that could be applied to the improvement of education. The child study movement provided the historical foundation for the field that became known as **educational psychology**. Unfortunately, the initial movement died by the end of the first decade of the 20th century, but psychologists persisted in seeking ways to improve education. And, perhaps more importantly, their efforts were a harbinger of the coming application of scientific psychology to practical problems of human concern. The stage was set for such professional fields as **clinical psychology**, **school psychology**, **industrial-organizational psychology**, and intelligence testing (See Chapter 4).

CLINICAL PSYCHOLOGY

In 1896, while working at the University of Pennsylvania, psychologist Lightner Witmer (1867–1956) agreed to see a boy who was experiencing difficulty in learning to spell. Witmer assumed that a spelling problem was a memory problem and reasoned that because memory is a mental process, psychology should have something to offer. His success with this and other cases led Witmer to establish a psychological clinic and to urge other psychologists to apply their knowledge to human problems and training programs that would prepare new psychologists for such work. In 1907, Witmer established a journal titled *The Psychological Clinic* and gave his efforts a name: *clinical psychology*. The Pennsylvania clinic pioneered the use of clinical teams that comprised physicians and social workers, specialists in vision and hearing, and psychologists, who worked together to evaluate cases and design remedial treatment. The clinic continued to grow. First serving only school children, it eventually began taking in other children as well as adults with a wide range of difficulties. Witmer's unique early work in application of psychological knowledge to practical problems earned him dual recognition: as the founder of clinical psychology and also as the founder of *school psychology*—an area of psychology that applies knowledge of clinical and educational psychology to the problems of children in schools.

At the same time that Witmer's Pennsylvania clinic was expanding, other psychologists interested in clinical applications were seeking professional identity and recognition. After meeting to discuss their concerns at the 1917 convention of the American Psychological Association (APA), a group of these clinicians formed the American Association of Clinical Psychologists—an organization that disbanded when the APA allowed it to become a recognized specialty under the the the APA umbrella. This was, however, an uneasy marriage because the APA was dominated by university psychologists at the time. The tension between clinicians and academicians grew during the 1930s, when the Great Depression resulted in competition between unemployed academic psychologists and clinical psychologists for applied jobs. The growing conflict led to the organization of the American Association for Applied Psychology—a group that existed until the end of World War II, when the APA reorganized its structure to include special interest divisions. The APA also expanded its statement of mission to include advancement of the profession and the promotion of human welfare. The clinicians had at last achieved recognition.

Prior to World War II, the role of clinical psychologists was mainly testing, evolving from intelligence testing to include personality testing during the 1930s. However, the war brought major changes. To begin with, it produced large increases in the need for psychotherapy among military personnel, and the APA began cooperating with universities, the Veterans Administration, and the U.S. Public Health Service to increase the pace of professional

An Early Clinician Leads the Way

One of the leaders of the movement to establish the American Association of Clinical Psychologists was Leta Stetter Hollingworth (1886–1939). A faculty member at Teachers College at Columbia University, Hollingworth had extensive experience working with children with intellectual disabilities. In 1914 she became the first psychologist appointed under the Civil Service in New York City, and by the time she completed her doctoral studies in 1916, she had already published several scientific articles. A popular and well respected clinical psychologist, she would later make a name for herself in advancing understanding of sex differences.

Leta Hollingworth was an activist on behalf of clinical psychology, and especially in pursuit of increased professional certification and recognition of clinical psychologists. She advocated for doctoral level training for clinicians, and she worked hard to push the APA to meet their needs. She also proposed that university psychology departments offer a special degree for clinicians, the Doctor of Psychology. Eventually, of course, the APA did establish a section for clinical psychology, but it was not until 1973 that the APA endorsed the Doctor of Psychology (Psy.D.) degree. Leta Hollingworth, who died of cancer at the age of 53, was a remarkable contributor to the discipline and certainly a leader ahead of her time.

Source: Hollingworth, H.L. 1990. *Leta Stetter Hollingworth: A Biography*. Bolton, Mass.: Anker Publishing (original work published 1943 by University of Nebraska Press).

clinical psychology training. Soon thereafter, in 1946, the APA began accrediting training programs in an effort to ensure their quality, and in 1949, adopted the **scientist-practitioner model** of training—an approach requiring a strong scientific foundation along with clinical skills training. In the years to follow, every American state would enact licensing requirements for clinical psychologists, and their numbers would dramatically increase. Today, clinical psychologists commonly use therapeutic techniques arising from behavioral, cognitive, psychodynamic, and humanistic perspectives. Ironically, despite their early difficulties finding a place in the APA, clinical psychologists today are a dominant force in the organization, and it is academic psychologists who are now forming alternative groups to meet their needs.

INDUSTRIAL-ORGANIZATIONAL PSYCHOLOGY

In 1902 Walter Dill Scott (1869–1955), one of the many early psychologists who had studied with Wilhelm Wundt, was a faculty member at Northwestern University in Chicago when a prominent advertising executive approached him to ask whether Scott would write a series of articles about the psychology of advertising. Although Scott had no real experience or education in advertising, he eventually wrote more than 30 articles and then collected them in two books on the subject. Scott believed that his understanding of basic psychological principles, coupled with his knowledge of experimental methods, made him suitable to contribute advice about advertising. Before long he established himself as an important voice in advertising, gained a faculty appointment as professor of advertising at Northwestern, and established his own company (the first of its kind) to provide consultation to industry.

German-born Hugo Münsterberg (1863–1916) was another of Wilhelm Wundt's students. In addition to his Leipzig Ph.D., he also earned a medical degree at the University of Heidelberg. At the invitation of William James, Münsterberg traveled to the United States in 1892, where he joined the faculty at Harvard University. After a brief return to Germany three years later, he went back to Harvard, where he remained for the rest of his life. He had a successful career that spanned a variety of interests in psychology, and he oversaw development of a new building for the psychology labs at Harvard. But in the early 1900s Münsterberg turned his attention to applications of his science, first in **forensic psychology** and abnormal psychology, and then in industrial psychology. In the latter field, his greatest interest was in improving worker selection

Read This!

You have no doubt seen advertisements that ask you to take a specific action to use a company's product: "Call Now for All Your Plumbing Needs!" or the Alka-Seltzer® plea to "Try it, you'll like it." A few years ago the Apple company asked us to "Think Different," and McDonald's would like us to "Wake up with a premium roast coffee." These are examples of *direct command* ads, an approach to marketing that suggests that the customer take a specific action. This approach was the brainchild of psychologist Walter Dill Scott, as was the *return coupon*. The return coupon also prompted the consumer to take a specific, direct action—in this case the action of clipping and returning a coupon to get a discount or a product.

Some advertisements are good enough to give us the sense that we are smelling the fresh-baked cookies or hearing the clear sounds from a high-tech speaker system. This kind of creative use of mental imagery to suggest sensory experiences associated with a product was also the product of Scott's imagination.

Source: Benjamin, L.T., Jr. 2007. *A Brief History of Modern Psychology*. Malden, Mass.: Blackwell Publishing.

and matching workers to jobs. He developed techniques for studying and simulating jobs so that he could test candidates for complex jobs in an effort to select those most likely to succeed.

The first person to earn a doctorate in the specialty of industrial psychology was Lillian Gilbreth, who completed her degree at Brown University in 1915. The wife of time-and-motion expert Frank Gilbreth, Lillian published a number of books jointly with her husband. Following Frank's premature death in 1924 and despite the challenges of managing a household with 12 children, Lillian Gilbreth continued her work. She began to tailor her interests toward design of environments for homemakers, giving attention to the details of the kitchen as a workplace and inventing a number of appliances and fixtures. If you find it handy to store bottles and other containers on the shelves that line the inside of your refrigerator door; if your kitchen appliances include an electric mixer; or if you have a trash container with a convenient foot pedal opener, you can thank Lillian Gilbreth—these are among the devices she invented and patented. She received many engineering awards and came to be known as the "mother of modern management." Two of her children, Frank Gilbreth, Jr., and Ernestine Gilbreth Carey, wrote bestselling books about their family life: *Cheaper By the Dozen* and *Bells On Their Toes*. Both books were eventually turned into movies: the former in 1950 (starring Clifton Webb) and the latter in 1952 (starring Myrna Loy).

The psychologists mentioned here are just a few of those who made significant contributions to the field of industrial-organizational psychology. Two others were behaviorist John B. Watson (Chapter 2), who left academic psychology and became quite successful in advertising, managing the accounts of a number of high-profile companies and making popular the idea of the coffee break (in an ad campaign for the Maxwell House Company); and Harry L. Hollingworth (1880–1956), husband of Leta Hollingworth, who became known for his research on the effectiveness of advertising following the 1913 publication of his book *Advertising and Selling*.

OTHER FACETS OF APPLIED PSYCHOLOGY

Psychologists have played an important role in many other areas of applied endeavor, in settings ranging from medical clinics to athletic fields and space capsules. Here we will touch upon just a few of those applications.

Human Factors

The special province of **human factors** psychology is the interface between people and machines, and especially the role of an understanding of human characteristics in the design of systems and machines. In designing a system, a human factors psychologist would be interested in which tasks a human can best perform and which a machine can best perform—arriving in turn at a human-machine interface with maximum efficiency and safety. Design and placement of aircraft and automobile controls, product design for appliances, and safety in workplaces like nuclear power plants are examples of the kinds of issues that interest human factors specialists. Today, human factors programs can be found both in university psychology departments and in engineering departments.

Sport Psychology

In the past few years, psychologists have found interesting research and practical applications in the study of sport and the behavior of people participating in sporting activities. These psychologists have investigated a wide range of interesting topics, including motivation, leadership, competition, cooperation, and the reciprocal relation between performance and psychological factors. Sports psychologists work with athletes to improve performance through the use of such techniques as mental imagery, attention focus, and stress management. They also study such interesting questions as whether the practice of "icing" a football kicker (calling timeout just before an opponent attempts a field goal) affects game performance, and whether the widely recognized "hot hand" (a lucky streak) in basketball is fact or fiction. Psychologists are finding the results of sport psychology research useful not only in athletic competition, but in other arenas as well (e.g., with performance artists).

Health Psychology

Many of the most pressing health problems of our time need not await more sophisticated or costly basic medical research. Instead, many of the most dangerous threats to our well-being—problems like lung cancer, obesity, chronic pain, sexually transmitted diseases—could be greatly diminished by effective programs of behavior change. This is the realm of health psychologists, whose careers are dedicated to the promotion of health and prevention of disease. Health psychologists can be found in the ranks of clinical practitioners, university researchers, and government policy analysts. All have in common the aim of improving quality of life by enhancing the health and well-being of people, whether individually or in groups.

Psychology and Law (Forensic Psychology)

Psychologists (such as Hugo Münsterberg) have long shown interest in the law. As early as the mid-19th century, an English court, after hearing the testimony of medical experts, pronounced an accused murderer not guilty by reason of insanity. And it was in 1954, while adjudicating the famous *Brown v. Board of Education* case, that the U.S. Supreme Court first accepted psychological science as evidence. The evidence in this case was research findings about racial identity and self-esteem, presented by psychologists Kenneth B. Clark and Mamie

Phipps Clark. After deliberating on these findings and other evidence, the Court struck down school segregation. Since the last quarter of the 20th century, psychological research and practice related to the law have dramatically increased. Psychologists have conducted important research on a variety of issues relevant to the law, including the limitations of eyewitness testimony, the dubious claims of repressed memory, the effects of pretrial publicity, and the dynamics of jury decision making. The increased interest in psychology and law has resulted in a number of joint psychology-law university programs offering graduate students both a law degree and a Ph.D. in psychology.

Environmental Psychology

We all have an interest in our connection to our environment—whether we are concerned with the immediate environment of our own bedroom or the relation between human behavior and global climate change. One of the most important developments in this hybrid field of **environmental psychology** was the establishment, in the 1940s, of the Midwest Psychological Field Station in a small town in Kansas. The key figure in this venture was social psychologist Roger Barker, whose research focus was in patterns of behavior-environment relations. For more than 20 years, the staff of the field station observed and recorded the behavior of ordinary people in many different community settings in an effort to understand behavior in its natural environments. Other researchers have conducted studies investigating the negative effects of noise, high temperatures, and crowding, as well as the stress created by disasters, whether natural (hurricanes, tornadoes, floods) or human-made (explosions at factories or oil rigs, nuclear power plant accidents). The real-world problems environmental psychologists study today also include the role of human behavior in contributing to, or reducing, natural challenges like energy conservation and climate change.

CAREERS IN PSYCHOLOGY

Although this chapter presents only a fraction of the number of opportunities awaiting those educated in the various subfields of psychology, it hopefully provides some indication of the tremendous possibilities for careers in the discipline. In this section we will examine career options of two types: those available to individuals with only a basic undergraduate (bachelor) degree in psychology and those requiring graduate training at the master's or doctoral level. As you will see, a talented student of psychology is limited only by the bounds of imagination and hard work.

Bachelor's Degree (B.A. or B.S.) Careers

Students who complete their college program with an undergraduate degree in psychology have many potential career options. However, this myriad of possibilities tends to be arrayed in two broad groupings: (1) work that is not directly connected to the field of psychology, but takes advantage of the skills of the psychology major; and (2) occupations more clearly and directly related to the professional field of psychology. Some of the most popular occupational areas for people with bachelor's degrees in psychology appear in *The College Majors' Handbook* (See Table 9.1).

Students seeking occupations that might seem clearly psychological in nature find jobs in mental health agencies, vocational counseling or rehabilitation, as psychological assistants, or as secondary school psychology teachers. More examples of psychology-related occupations appear in Table 9.2.

Although many students find interesting careers in psychology-related fields, many others find their skills useful in a broad range of jobs beyond the confines of those areas normally considered "psychology." Thus, psychology graduates may work in hotel management, human resources, technical writing, college admissions, and many other, similar positions. Additional occupations, perhaps not clearly psychological in nature, but appropriate to the skills of psychology majors, appear in Table 9.3

You may wonder what it is about psychology students that would prepare them for such a varied group of job possibilities, making them desirable candidates for work that most people might not associate with the field of psychology. It may be obvious to some that students of psychology should have some

---

TABLE 9.1
Some of the Top 10 Career Opportunities for Students with a Bachelor's Degree in Psychology

- Labor Relations, Training, & Personnel
- Marketing
- Other Administrative Jobs
- Other Management Occupations
- Real Estate, Business Services, Insurance
- Sales
- Social Work
- Top- and Mid-Level Management and Administration

Source: Fogg, N.P., P.E. Harrington, and T.F. Harrington. 2004. The College Majors' Handbook. Indianapolis, Ind.: JIST Works, Inc

TABLE 9.2
A Sample of Psychology-Related Job Opportunities for Students with Bachelor's Degrees

- Alcohol/Drug Abuse Counselor
- Career Counselor
- Child Care Worker
- Corrections Officer
- Family Services Worker
- Housing/Student Life Coordinator
- Mental Health Technician
- Parole Officer
- Radio/TV Research Assistant

Source: Landrum, E.R., and S.F. Davis. 2003. The Psychology Major: Career Options and Strategies for Success, 2nd ed. Upper Saddle River, N.J.: Pearson-Prentice Hall.

ability to understand and work with others. Although that may well be true, it is also true that good psychology students have problem solving skills, a capacity for critical thinking, and some understanding of the methods of research and quantitative analysis. They have experience in organizing and presenting written and oral communications, and they often have research skills. In defining the **psychological literacy** that students in the field should develop, a recent APA workgroup on undergraduate education created the following list of desirable skills:

- a well-defined vocabulary and basic knowledge of the critical subject matter of psychology
- an appreciation for the intellectual challenges required to use scientific thinking and the disciplined analysis of information to evaluate alternative courses of action
- a creative and amiable skeptic approach to problem solving
- an ability to apply psychological principles to personal, social, and organizational issues in work, relationships, and the broader community
- professional ethics
- competence in using and evaluating information and technology

TABLE 9.3

A Sample of Occupations Relevant to Psychology Majors' Skills but Not Directly Psychology-Related

- Advertising Agent
- Camp Staff Director
- Community Organizer
- Customer Relations
- Educational Coordinator
- Intelligence Officer
- Loan Officer
- Property Management
- Technical Writer

Source: Landrum, E.R., and S.F. Davis. 2003. The Psychology Major: Career Options and Strategies for Success, 2nd ed. Upper Saddle River, N.J.: Pearson-Prentice Hall.

- the ability to communicate effectively in different modes and with many different audiences
- a capacity for recognizing, understanding, and fostering respect for diversity
- a capacity for being insightful and reflective about one's own and others' behaviors and mental processes

Undergraduate education in psychology is versatile, adaptable, and applicable to nearly any human (and many animal) service setting, and it prepares many students for satisfying lifelong careers. And for those who aspire to become psychologists, an undergraduate degree in the field provides the preparation required to continue their education at the graduate level.

Graduate Level Careers (Master's and Doctoral Degrees)

For those with advanced degrees, psychology is a growing field. About 12,000 of the students who complete graduate degrees in psychology each year in the United States earn master's degrees. A typical master's program requires about two years of full-time study, usually in a specialized area of psychology, although some universities offer master's degrees in general psychology. The training program often includes a requirement for an independent research project (thesis), and many students in master's programs complete required internship or practicum experiences. For some students, the master's degree (usually Master of Arts or Master of Science) is preparation for doctoral studies, but for many it is the last step before seeking careers in the field. Students who have achieved the master's level may conduct therapeutic or testing activities under supervision of a doctoral level psychologist; they may work in schools (as school psychologists or counselors); they may work in human service agencies serving persons with mental health problems or intellectual disabilities; or they may work in private business or government offices.

Students who choose to pursue doctoral programs may expect to spend a total of five or six years in additional study beyond the bachelor's degree. There are, of course, many possible areas of specialization in doctoral studies in psychology—the APA has 54 divisions, many of them representing specialty areas in the field. Realistically, most doctoral programs can be grouped into about 15 subfields (See Table 9.4).

Students who expect to seek university or research jobs usually work toward a Doctor of Philosophy (Ph.D.) degree, and a significant portion of their studies is devoted to completion of a major original research project, the dissertation. Whether the aim is to work in applied clinical areas or in academic settings, the preparation of Ph.D. students involves a significant focus on research methodology and the empirical foundations of psychology. Those in specialties like clinical or counseling psychology will also complete a year-long internship. Doctoral students whose career aim is primarily clinical application may study

TABLE 9.4
Subfields of Psychology in Which Doctoral Degrees Are Offered

• Clinical	• Cognitive
• Community	• Counseling
• Developmental	• Educational
• Experimental	• Forensic
• Health	• Industrial-Organizational
• Neuropsychology	• Psychometric/Quantitative
• Rehabilitation	• School
• Social	• Sport

Source: Zwolinski, J. 2010. Careers in Psychology. In D.G. Myers, Psychology, 9th ed. New York: Worth Publishers. A1–A11. , 2010.

for the Doctor of Psychology (Psy.D.) degree and will spend a much greater amount of their time in supervised clinical work, with a correspondingly lesser focus on research work. Individuals wishing to practice psychology must not only meet educational requirements (usually a doctoral degree), but must also meet the licensure requirements of their respective states. According to the U.S. Department of Education, approximately 5,000 people in the United States currently earn doctorates in psychology each year. Of these, more than 70 percent are women.

The American Psychological Association and the British Psychological Society are among the sources of information available on careers in psychology for individuals who have earned doctoral degrees. The following Websites provide helpful resources about careers in the field:

> http://www.apa.org
> http://www.bps.org.uk
> http://www.psychwww.com/careers/masters.htm
> http://psychology.about.com/od/careersinpsychology/a/careersbach.htm

CONCLUSION

In its earliest days psychology was primarily an experimental science, but from the early 20th century onward, interest grew in useful applications of psychological knowledge. Early applications included efforts to assist children in educational settings, adults and children in clinical settings, and advertisers and marketers. As clinical psychology gained a foothold, its practitioners sought recognition from organized psychology, including the APA. Meaningful recognition came following World War II, which propelled the need for therapeutic applications of psychology. Applications of psychology have continued to expand, now encompassing such diverse areas as the law, sports, marketing, and the interface between humans and machines.

For individuals with psychology degrees (at all academic levels), the range of career possibilities is broad—not only in occupations that are clearly psychology related, but also in a variety of work settings involving people in many ways. And if your goal is to work as a psychologist, graduate studies in the field offer an equally broad field to choose from, ranging from research to clinical and counseling applications, tests and measurements, and more. A strong foundation in psychology is a key to effective critical, methodological, quantitative, and decision-making skills. The field is diverse, and the opportunities rich.

CHAPTER 10

SUMMING UP:
PSYCHOLOGY IN PERSPECTIVE

As we near the end of our overview of the field of psychology, it seems appropriate to attempt to put into perspective the highlights of the journey we have made through the history and the points of view that define this fascinating discipline. We have seen that psychology has a very long past, perhaps dating back to prehistoric times. Indeed, many of the research questions that modern psychological scientists pursue originated with philosophers and physiologists who predated the establishment of Wilhelm Wundt's laboratory in 1879. Some of these early scholars made significant contributions to an understanding of human behavior, and others left us with questions that persist even today. René Descartes, for example, in trying to understand the connection between the mind and reflexes, left us with the yet-unresolved problem of mind-body dualism.

Despite having roots in antiquity, psychology as an organized, coherent field is a relatively new discipline. And it was the outstanding laboratory scientists of the 19th century who began to shed light on questions that laid the groundwork for this new science. Examples abound, beginning with research like Fechner's investigation of psychophysics and von Helmholtz's discovery of the speed of nerve signal transmission. Then, as experimental psychology developed, Wundt and his followers began empirical investigation of the kinds of questions philosophers had been asking for centuries—questions about the nature of consciousness, perception, and the structure of the mind. Wundt's students not only pushed forward the agenda of an experimental science, but also went on to establish psychology as an applied field, both in the early treatment of clinical problems and in the first efforts to use psychological science in the realm of business.

As the field evolved, the early centers of growth were in Europe and in America. In Vienna, physician Sigmund Freud developed the interest in intrapsychic conflict and neuroses that would eventually make his name a household word. Although his work would be severely criticized by other scientists, Freud believed his approach was scientific and doggedly pursued and promoted his vision of psychoanalysis. In the early 20th century Freud's fame reached the shores of North America. Although he visited the United States only once, his impact on American psychology was a force to be reckoned with.

In the United States, the structuralist psychology of E.B. Titchener and his followers was on the wane by the 1920s, challenged by functionalism, a distinctly American perspective. Stemming from the work of William James, functionalism brought an interest not in the structure of consciousness, but in the functions it might serve in the lives of people. Functionalism produced important laboratory work in such centers as Columbia University and the University of Chicago and helped to launch the careers of such luminaries as John Dewey, who went on to become one of America's most important philosophers.

It was John B. Watson who dramatically moved the field from the functionalism of William James in the direction of an extreme empirical focus on observable behavior. Watson began applying behavior principles to such phenomena as childhood fears, and although many criticized his behaviorism as too simplistic or rigid in its application to child behavior, he nevertheless developed a popular following among parents. Watson was not the only researcher committed to a rigorous scientific understanding of behavior. In Russia, Ivan Pavlov, using dogs as subjects, was studying the reflexive learning that would become known to the world as classical conditioning. Ultimately, the Pavlovian model would become the basis for important therapeutic techniques, most notably systematic desensitization, that remain in use today.

Further advances in the behavioral approach emerged from the work of American B.F. Skinner, who viewed much of the psychology of earlier psychologists with a critical eye and deemed most of it (especially psychoanalysis) unscientific. He particularly objected to the focus of other scientists on averaged data from groups of research subjects—his **functional behavior analysis** reflected a more precise understanding of individual behavior.

Recognizing that Pavlov's focus on reflexive behavior could not adequately account for much of animal and human behavior, Skinner undertook rigorous study of individual animals, aiming to build an **inductive** science—developing general principles from a study of individual cases. Skinner vowed, early in his career, to remake psychology to his liking, and he spent the rest of his long life doing just that. Inevitably, there were psychologists who believed the behaviorists had gone too far in the direction of an insistence on the study of observable behavior. The behaviorists could not, their critics argued, adequately account for many psychological phenomena—language, memory, thinking, problem solving, and other cognitive processes. Despite the objections of behaviorists, the cognitive psychologists began to hypothesize the existence of such cognitive structures as schemata, scripts, and cognitive maps as aids to human and animal learning and perception. The cognitive movement also led to efforts to apply computer models to an understanding of intelligence, decision making, and other human-like functions.

While cognitive psychologists were attempting to "get into the heads" of their research subjects, another perspective, also critical of behaviorism, arose in the form of humanistic psychology. Led by Carl Rogers, the humanistic approach placed emphasis on the feelings and self-views of individuals. The humanists gave us much of the common language associated with the self, most notably the idea of self-concept. Humanistic psychology became known as the Third Force, in recognition of its effort to provide an alternative to behaviorism and psychoanalysis.

Not content to invent hypothetical internal structures to account for behavior, behavioral neuroscientists have devoted themselves to studying and understanding the relation between the nervous system and behavior. Building on the work of earlier scientists, including the 19th-century German physiologists, biopsychological researchers have expanded our understanding of the neuron, the brain, and the brain-body connection. Contemporary neuroscientists have made some remarkable strides, not only in basic knowledge of the nervous system, but also in development of techniques and devices that hold the promise of providing remediation and treatment of serious neurological and neuromuscular diseases.

In the last few decades of the 20th century, psychologists came to realize that research and practice in many areas have been less than sensitive to the social and cultural backgrounds of many of the people whom they study. And they have discovered that some time-honored psychological processes may not be as universally experienced as we may have once believed—that, instead, they may be experienced differently in different cultural settings. Psychologists using a sociocultural approach seek to develop a psychology of all people—not simply a North American or European American psychology.

All these perspectives, and others we do not have space to examine in this book, have contributed to the amazing growth of the field of psychology. When the APA was founded in 1892, 26 psychologists (all men) attended the first meeting at Clark University. Today the organization has more than 150,000 members, and about 70 percent of new doctoral degrees are earned by women. These psychologists not only continue to conduct important research in many different fields of interest, bringing a variety of approaches to bear upon their research problems, but they are also finding a mind-boggling array of novel areas of application for their science. It is unlikely that any of the 26 original members of the APA could have foreseen the robust, diverse discipline that exists today.

Nearly 60 years ago, B.F. Skinner argued that "The methods of science have been enormously successful wherever they have been tried. Let us then apply them to human affairs." Today, the wisdom of that advice is evident in the diversity of science and practice we see in modern day psychology.

GLOSSARY

analytical psychology Carl Jung's version of psychoanalysis, which included the notion of a collective unconscious and less emphasis on sex, which was a dominant feature in the psychology of Sigmund Freud.

anterograde amnesia Inability to acquire new memories following a traumatic or pathological event (e.g., a brain injury); distinguished from retrograde amnesia, which is inability to retrieve memories that existed before such an event.

anxiety A feeling of apprehension, often accompanied by physiological changes, such as increased heart rate, sweating, etc.

artificial intelligence A field of study that involves programming computers to behave intelligently.

association cortex The parts of the cerebral cortex that combine sensory and motor information and thus enable the brain to perform complex cognitive tasks.

associationism A philosophic viewpoint that studies how relationships form between ideas and experiences.

attribution The assignment of causes to behavior of other people and ourselves.

axon An extension of a nerve cell that carries impulses from the cell body to other nerve cells.

axon terminal The end of an axon that forms a synapse on another neuron.

basic anxiety According to psychoanalyst Karen Horney, the fear and insecurity arising from children's dependence upon their parents.

behavior modification   Application of operant conditioning principles to change behavior.

behavior therapy   Application of learning principles, often classical conditioning, to eliminate undesired behaviors.

behaviorism   A psychological perspective based on observable relationships between behavior and environment and rejecting causal explanations that use unobservable psychological constructs or processes.

biological psychology (*also* biopsychology, behavioral neuroscience, physiological psychology)   A psychological perspective based upon study of the relation between biology and behavior.

brain   The part of the central nervous system, contiguous with the upper end of the spinal cord, that contains the nerve centers that receive sensory input and produce motor impulses. The brain is a complex biochemical system, composed (in humans) of approximately 100 billion nerve cells, and reacting via electrochemical mechanisms with the environment and the body.

Broca's area   An area of the left frontal lobe of the brain that controls muscle movements necessary for speech.

catharsis   The psychoanalytic notion that a person can achieve release of emotional energy through insight into unconscious causes or through action (e.g., aggression).

cell body (soma)   The portion of a neuron (nerve cell) containing the nucleus and the cell's maintenance structures.

central nervous system   The brain and spinal cord.

cerebellum   A part of the hindbrain involved in central control of movement.

cerebral hemisphere   The right or left half of the cerebral cortex, the outermost part of the forebrain.

classical conditioning (Pavlovian conditioning)   Type of associative learning in which a neutral stimulus, after repeated pairing with a reflex-eliciting unconditioned stimulus, may elicit a similar response. The initial stimulus and reflex are known as the unconditional stimulus (UCS) and unconditional response (UCR); after pairing, the neutral stimulus becomes a conditional stimulus (CS), and its accompanying response becomes a conditional response (CR).

client-centered therapy   A nondirective approach to psychotherapy that allows a client to explore personal issues without judgment or direction by the therapist. A product of the humanistic psychology of Carl Rogers.

clinical psychology   A psychological specialty dealing with the study, evaluation, and treatment of individuals with psychological disorders.

cognitive-behavioral perspective   An approach that combines cognitive therapy (dealing with patterns of thinking) with behavior therapy (dealing with overt behavior).

cognitive map   A mental representation of the features of an individual's environment.

cognitive psychology   A subfield of psychology concerned with the mental processes involved in such activities as problem solving, language, memory, perception, and information processing.

cognitive science   A field of study that encompasses the study of mental processes in such areas as cognitive psychology,   cultural anthropology, linguistics, epistemology, and artificial intelligence.

collective unconscious   According to Carl Jung, an inherited mind structure handed down via evolution and containing traces of the experiences of ancestors, both human and nonhuman.

conditional response (CR)   In the classical conditioning model, a response to a previously neutral stimulus, which occurs due to pairing of the previously neutral stimulus (CS) with an unconditional stimulus (UCS).

conditional stimulus (CS)   In the classical conditioning model, a stimulus that does not naturally elicit a reflexive response, but which can come to elicit a response through pairing with a naturally effective (unconditional) stimulus.

connectionism   An explanation for learning that focuses on the connection between a stimulus situation and a response, with the assumption that repetition strengthens the connection. This viewpoint is associated with the work of E.L. Thorndike.

consciousness   Awareness of oneself and the environment.

contiguity   Proximity in time and space between a stimulus situation and a response. The role of contiguity was a central feature in the learning theory of E.R. Guthrie.

contingency   An "if-then" relationship between two events (such as an operant behavior and its consequence) in which one event (i.e., the consequence) depends upon occurrence of the other event (behavior). Contingency analysis is key to the behavioral approach of B.F. Skinner.

corpus callosum   A large web of nerve fibers connecting the right and left hemispheres of the brain, allowing communication between them.

correlation   The extent to which two or more variables or measures are related to one another. Often expressed statistically as a *correlation coefficient*.

cortex (cerebral cortex)   The layer of neural tissue covering the hemispheres of the forebrain and comprising the centers of higher cognitive processes.

counterconditioning   A technique that behavior therapists use to assist a client to make new, desired   responses to a stimulus that evokes undesired behaviors.

cross-cultural psychologist   Psychological scientist who studies similarities and differences in social and psychological characteristics of people across multiple cultures.

cultural anthropology   A branch of anthropology devoted to study of such cultural characteristics as language, attitudes, beliefs, and customs, and their relation to environment.

culture   The shared way of life of a group, including behaviors, values, and beliefs that the group passes on from one generation to the next.

declarative memory   Information that a person can recall and discuss. Distinct from procedural or implicit memory (e.g., how to dance or ride a bicycle), which is more difficult to express verbally.

defense mechanism   According to psychoanalytic theory, the methods by which individuals unconsciously alter their perceptions of reality in order to reduce anxiety and protect the ego.

dendrite   A branching structure extending from the cell body of a neuron to synapses, where the dendrite receives messages from other nerve cells.

depolarization   Reduction in the difference between the negatively charged inside of a neuron and the positively charged outside, taking place when the potassium and sodium ions inside and outside the cell exchange places.

depression   A mental state characterized by pessimism, lack of energy and activity, negative self-thoughts, and negative mood.

desensitization   Decreasing a response (such as a phobia) to a stimulus through repeated exposure to the stimulus. When used therapeutically, desensitization is often accompanied by such ancillary techniques as relaxation training.

developmental psychology   A subfield of psychology that includes study of physical, behavioral, and cognitive changes across the life span.

dispositional attribution   Explanation of behavior based upon internal personality characteristics.

dualism   Belief in a clear divide between mind and body. Often associated with the philosophy of René Descartes (i.e., *Cartesian dualism*).

educational psychology   A subfield of psychology concerned with study and application of mental and behavioral processes to learning in educational settings.

ego   According to Sigmund Freud, the personality structure mediating among the id, the superego, and the limits of reality.

electrochemical   Dealing with the role of electricity in chemical changes. The transmission of nerve impulses is an electrochemical process.

emic   A culture-specific psychological principle or process.

emotional intelligence   Ability to recognize, understand, manage, and use emotions in interactions with others.

empathy   Ability to understand and share the emotional and cognitive perspective of another person.

empiricism   Philosophic perspective based on the belief that our understanding of the world arises from sensory experience.

environmental psychology   A multidisciplinary field that studies the relationship between people and their habitats and environments.

epistemology   Area within philosophy concerned with the study of the origin and nature of knowledge.

ethnocentrism   Universal tendency to judge other cultures from the viewpoint of one's own culture.

etic   A universal psychological principle or process.

eugenics   A social philosophy aiming to improve the genetic constitution of people through selective breeding. Those pursuing the aims of eugenics were responsible for the involuntary sterilization of people with intellectual disabilities and other devalued groups for more than half of the 20th century.

evolutionary theory   A viewpoint, deriving from the work of Charles Darwin, that human behavior is the product of natural selection and can be understood in the context of the process of evolution.

existentialism   A philosophical movement focusing on individual experience and the responsibility of the individual to assume responsibility for his or her own behavior.

experimental psychology   Field of psychological science conducting research in controlled situations to gain knowledge about behavior and mental processes.

explanatory style   Approach an individual uses to explain behavior in terms of causes; this approach is characterized along such dimensions as internal-external, global-specific, and stable-unstable.

expressive aphasia   Lack of capacity to speak in a meaningful way, often as a result of damage to *Broca's area* in the brain.

extinction   Reduction or elimination of a response, occurring in operant conditioning when a behavior is not reinforced; in classical conditioning, extinction occurs when a conditional stimulus is no longer followed by an unconditional stimulus.

forebrain   Forward part of the brain, including the cerebral hemispheres and other key brain structures.

forensic psychology   Application of psychological theories and techniques to the law.

free association   Psychoanalytic technique intended to reveal the unconscious. The client relaxes and describes whatever thoughts come to mind.

frontal cortex (frontal lobe)   The front part of the cerebral cortex, involved in motor control and *executive functions* (planning, abstract thinking, coordination of goal-oriented behavior).

functional behavior analysis   Analysis of the relation between operant behavior and the reinforcers and stimulus events that control it.

functional Magnetic Resonance Imaging (fMRI)   Portrayal of brain activity by successive computer-generated images produced through use of radio waves and magnetic fields.

functionalism   Early 20th-century American school of psychology that studied the functions of consciousness and behavior for human adaptation and survival.

gene   A length of DNA that, by encoding information for construction of proteins, provides a blueprint for human or animal development. The physical unit of heredity.

health psychology (behavioral medicine)   Branch of psychology studying and applying psychological principles and influences to health-related behaviors and conditions.

hierarchy of needs   A model of human motivation developed by Abraham Maslow; it assumes that basic physiological needs must be satisfied before such higher-level needs as safety or belonging. At the apex of the model is self-actualization.

hindbrain   A part of the brain located near the back and bottom of the skull. The hindbrain includes such structures as the cerebellum, medulla, and pons, and regulates such functions as heartrate, breathing, balance, and sleep.

hippocampus   Brain structure important in processing declarative (usually verbal) and spatial memories.

human factors psychology   An area of psychology concerned with the interactions of people, machines, and physical environments.

humanistic psychology   Psychology's so-called "Third Force," formed as a reaction to behaviorism and psychoanalysis, with a focus on free will, meaning, and self-actualization.

hypothetical construct   A concept or entity assumed to lie within the person and which represents or explains a relation between such observable events as stimuli and responses but is not itself directly observable. Common examples of hypothetical constructs include anxiety, personality, and habit.

hypothetico-deductive approach   An approach to research often associated with the work of Clark L. Hull and involving development (deduction) of testable hypotheses from theory. Depending on results of research, hypothesis testing may either support the theory or reveal a need for change in the theory.

hysteria   Psychoanalytic term referring to a condition in which psychological conflict is assumed to be converted to physical symptoms (e.g., paralysis, loss of vision). The modern term for this condition is *conversion disorder*. The condition is rather rare, making up no more than two percent of diagnoses.

id   According to Sigmund Freud, the part of the personality that tries to satisfy the biological drives of aggression and sex.

ideal self   In the humanistic psychology perspective, an individual's view of the way he or she would like to be.

independent self-construal   A view of self that is predicated on unique personal characteristics and individual aspirations.

individual differences   Psychological approach dedicated to the study of dimensions and characteristics that distinguish people from one another.

individual psychology   A psychoanalytic perspective put forth by Alfred Adler and emphasizing personal goals and social aspects of development.

individualism-collectivism   A cultural dimension that describes the people of a group along a continuum from a focus on individual goals and personal characteristics (individualism) to an emphasis on group goals and one's relationship to the group (collectivism).

inductive science   Scientific reasoning that proceeds from specific individual observations to formulation of general principles. Associated in earlier times with Francis Bacon and in the 20th century with B.F. Skinner.

industrial-organizational psychology   A branch of psychology that applies psychological principles and methods to the behavior of people in the workplace.

inferiority complex   According to Alfred Adler, the tendency for human behavior to be motivated by self-perceptions of deficiency or inferiority.

intelligence   Cognitive abilities enabling an individual to adapt, learn from experience, solve problems, and acquire new skills.

intelligence quotient (IQ)   A method for standardizing measures of intelligence, originally calculated by dividing mental age by chronological age and multiplying the quotient by 100 (MA/CA X 100). Today psychologists define the intelligence quotient as a *deviation IQ*, which is calculated statistically depending on the location of an individual score in a distribution adjusted to an average of 100.

interdependent self-construal   A self-view defined in terms of relationship to others (family, friends, co-workers, etc.)

ion   An electrically charged atom. The passage of potassium and sodium ions across the cell membrane is instrumental in the transmission of nerve signals.

latent content   In Sigmund Freud's psychoanalytic perspective, latent content is the hidden or underlying meaning of a dream.

latent learning   Learning that has occurred (generally through experience or environmental factors)) but is not observable. Latent learning was important to the learning theory of E.L. Thorndike.

law of effect   The principle, proposed by Thorndike, that effective problem-solving behaviors are strengthened whereas ineffective behaviors are weakened.

law of exercise   The principle, proposed by Thorndike, that connections learned between stimuli and responses are strengthened by practice.

libido   A psychoanalytic term denoting life energy directed toward sex.

linguistics   The scientific study of language, including its structure, meaning, and sounds.

locus of control   A term referring to individuals' perception of personal control over life events. People who believe that they exert control over life events have an internal locus of control; those who believe events are controlled by luck, fate, or powerful others have an external locus of control.

long-term/short-term orientation   A cultural dimension describing a culture's perspective on the importance of the future versus the present and past.

magnetoencephalography (MEG)   A technique used to map brain activity by monitoring the magnetic fields generated by the natural electrical activity of the neurons of the brain.

manifest content   According to Sigmund Freud, the obvious, or remembered, content of a dream.

masculinity-femininity   A cultural dimension indicating the extent to which a culture values traditional gender roles and such traits as assertiveness and competitiveness (masculine) or more egalitarian roles and relationships (feminine).

mental age   Mental ability level of a child, in terms of the age level at which a typical child would show the same ability (e.g., an eight-year-old with the ability of a typical ten-year-old has a mental age of ten years). The term *mental age* derives from the work of Alfred Binet, who called it mental level.

mesmerism   The forerunner of hypnotism, named for Franz Mesmer, who claimed he could treat disorders via magnetism.

midbrain   A small brain area between the forebrain and hindbrain that forms part of the brainstem and connects the spinal cord to the forebrain. Plays a role in control of movement and vision.

mirror neurons   Nerve cells in the frontal lobe that are active when a person observes the behavior of another person and facilitate imitation and understanding of others.

moral anxiety   According to Freudian theory, the fear of negative self-evaluation arising from failure to meet the standards of the superego

motor cortex   A brain area located at the back of the frontal lobes of the cortex and responsible for voluntary movement.

motor neuron   Nerve cell carrying signals from the central nervous system to muscles or glands.

multicultural psychologist   One who studies multiple cultural groups in the same broad context, such as ethnic minority groups within the United States.

multiple intelligence   The theory that intelligence encompasses not only the abilities measured by traditional IQ tests (e.g., quantitative and verbal skills) but also a range of additional skills (e.g., musical, spatial, interpersonal).

myelin   A layer of fatty protein covering the axon fibers of many neurons, insulating the axon and enhancing transmission of nerve impulses.

negative symptoms   Symptoms of schizophrenia characterized by reduction or absence of normal behavior. Examples include apathy, decreased emotion, and poverty of speech.

nerve tracts   A bundle of neural fibers in the central nervous system.

neuromodulator   A chemical acting at the synapse to enhance or weaken the effects of other neurotransmitters.

neuron   The basic building block of the nervous system; a nerve cell.

neurotic anxiety   Anxiety that, according to Sigmund Freud, arises from the id and is an unconscious fear that the libido will take control at an inappropriate time.

neurotransmitter   A chemical released from an axon terminal that crosses the synaptic gap and binds to a receptor site on the dendrite of another neuron, influencing the tendency of the receiving neuron to fire.

nondirective therapy   (*see* client-centered therapy)

nucleus   The central component of a neuron, controlling reproduction and metabolism of the cell, and containing the cell's genetic material.

objective anxiety   Anxiety occurring in response to a real threat from the environment.

occipital lobe   The part of the cerebral cortex of each brain hemisphere located at the rear of the brain and receiving input from visual fields.

operant behavior   Behavior that *operates* on the environment and produces consequences. B.F. Skinner identified and named operant behavior.

operant conditioning   Learning occurring when consequences strengthen (reinforce) or weaken (punish) the behavior they follow.

paradigm   A broad theory or model that defines the general approach to research in an area of study.

parasympathetic bervous system   The autonomic nervous system division that calms the body.

parietal lobe   The part of the cerebral cortex located behind the frontal lobe and above the occipital lobe; processes input for touch, body position, and objects in space.

peak experience   A brief experience of clarity, joy, insight, or feelings of accomplishment—a sense of self-actualization, according to humanistic psychologist Abraham Maslow.

personalized system of instruction (PSI)   A self-paced, mastery-based approach to teaching and learning. Behaviorist Fred S. Keller developed PSI in the 1960s.

physiology   A branch of biology that studies the physical and chemical aspects of the activity and function of the body. One of the sciences that gave rise to psychology in the 19th century.

pleasure principle   In Sigmund Freud's psychoanalytic theory, the motivation to gratify basic biological drives, arising from the id.

positron emission tomography (PET)   A visual scanning technique that allows creation of images of the brain or other organs and tracks activity by analyzing absorption of a radioactive glucose substance.

positive symptoms   Symptoms of schizophrenia that constitute an addition to normal behavior. Examples include hallucinations, disorganized thinking, and delusions.

post-reinforcement pause   In operant conditioning, the pause in responding that occurs after the learner receives reinforcement and before the behavior resumes.

power distance   A cultural dimension that reflects the extent to which a group accepts unequal levels of power or control among individuals within the group.

procedural memory   Memory for how to *do* things—usually nonverbal—like riding a bicycle.

projective test   A test that requires the individual to respond to ambiguous stimuli (e.g., pictures or inkblots) and, according to psychoanalysts, reveals the underlying dynamics of personality.

psychoanalysis   A personality theory and approach to psychotherapy developed by Sigmund Freud and based on the belief that individual behaviors, feelings, and thoughts come from unconscious conflicts and motivation.

psychodynamic psychology   A perspective and a therapeutic approach based on psychoanalysis and assuming the importance of unconscious motives.

psychological literacy   An understanding of the vocabulary and principles of psychology, and the ability to apply critical thinking to the use of terms and principles.

psychology   The science of behavior and mental processes.

psychoneurosis (neurosis)   A disorder involving feelings of distress and deficits in functioning that are not psychotic in nature and are not due to physiological causes.

psychophysics   The study of the relation between physical characteristics of stimuli and the perception of stimuli. Derives from the work of such 19th-century German scientists as Gustav Fechner and Ernst Weber.

purposive behaviorism   In the learning theory of E.C. Tolman, the view that learning was goal directed.

reality principle   In psychoanalysis, the process the ego uses to temper the desires of the id within the boundaries of the reality of the situation.

reciprocal determinism   In the social learning theory of Albert Bandura, the mutual influence occurring among an individual's behavior, characteristics (cognitions), and external environment.

reflex   An automatic, unlearned response to a stimulus. Examples include construction of the pupil of the eye in response to light or the patellar (knee-jerk) response to physical stimulation.

refractory period   The brief period following firing of a neuron, during which the cell cannot fire again until its chemistry is restored.

replication   Repeating a research study, often under different circumstances or with different participants, in an effort to verify the findings and their generality.

repression   In psychoanalytic theory, the exclusion from consciousness any thoughts, memories, or feelings that might provoke anxiety.

resistance   According to psychoanalysis, the tendency for patients to block transfer of information to consciousness from the unconscious.

schedules of reinforcement   In behavioral research, the pattern or program by which reinforcing consequences are delivered following the occurrence of operant behaviors. The concept derives from the work of B.F. Skinner.

schema   According to cognitive psychologists, a mental framework or representation of an object or category that aids the processing of information.

schizophrenia   Potentially severe mental disorder characterized by inappropriate behaviors and emotions, perceptual disturbances, delusions, and disorganized thought patterns.

school psychology   An area of psychology that applies knowledge of clinical and educational psychology to the problems of children in schools.

scientist-practitioner model   An approach to doctoral level training in clinical psychology that emphasizes not only clinical work, but also a strong background in research skills.

script   A cognitive representation of the sequence of components of a complex behavior.

self   The whole of personality and the behaviors, mental processes, and feelings that contribute to individual identity

self-actualization   According to humanistic psychologist Abraham Maslow, achievement of the full experience of individual potential and talents.

self-efficacy   The extent to which individuals believe they can accomplish goals or influence events affecting them.

sensory cortex   An area of the cerebral cortex located at the front of the parietal lobe and receiving sensory information for touch and bodily movement.

sensory neuron   Nerve cells carrying information from sensory receptors to the central nervous system.

serial position effect   The tendency to better remember material at the beginning and end of a list than items in the middle.

situational attribution   Assignment of cause for a behavior to specific aspects of an individual's environment.

social cognition   Study of influences affecting processing of information in a social context, and their effect on social behavior.

social learning   Acquisition of social behavior through observation and imitation of others. Associated with the work of Albert Bandura.

social psychology   The area of psychology that involves study of the social interaction of people and the influence of the presence of others on the behaviors and mental processes of individuals.

sociocultural approach   A perspective that recognizes the role of environment, including culture, in development of people and their mental processes and behaviors.

somatic nervous system (skeletal nervous system)   The division of the peripheral nervous system that controls the skeletal muscles of the body.

spinal cord   A column of nerve tissue connected to the brain and extending downward through holes in the vertebrae. The spinal cord transmits messages to and from the brain and initiates and coordinates reflexes.

sport psychology   Branch of psychology studying and applying psychological principles and findings to athletic activity, often with the goal of improving performance.

statistical significance   A statistical judgment about the likelihood that an obtained result occurred by chance and, by inference, whether findings for a sample of participants also exist in the broader population.

stereotyping   Judging a person based on a generalized belief about a group to which the person belongs. Although stereotypes can be accurate, they often are not.

stream of consciousness   The natural flow of thoughts, emotions, sensations, and other material constituting human consciousness. A concept popularized by William James.

structuralism   A school of psychological thought dedicated to the study of the structure of consciousness through the introspection (self-examination) of carefully trained observers. Structuralism reached its height in the late 19th and early 20th century under the leadership of Edward Titchener.

superego   In the psychology of Sigmund Freud, the personality structure reflecting ideals and moral standards. Often considered similar to the modern concept of conscience.

synapse   The junction including an axon terminal of a sending nerve cell and the dendrite or cell body of a receiving neuron. This unit allows transmission of a nerve signal across the synaptic gap from one neuron to the next.

synaptic gap   The tiny space between the axon terminal of a neuron and the dendrite or cell body of another nerve cell. Neurotransmitters cross this gap to stimulate the receiving cell.

temporal lobe   One of the lobes of the cerebral cortex, located near the ear in each hemisphere and receiving auditory information from the ears.

token economy   A behavioral training system in which desired operant behaviors result in rewards (tokens) that can be changed for other reinforcers (e.g., food, privileges, merchandise). Token economies have proven useful in a variety of human service and educational settings.

uncertainty avoidance   A cultural dimension reflecting the extent to which members of a group experience anxiety in ambiguous situations and develop cultural ways to avoid such situations.

unconditional positive regard   Care for and interest in another person independent of the person's behavior, attitudes, or feelings. A central component of the therapeutic approach of Carl Rogers.

unconditional response (UCR)   Any reflexive behavior that occurs without specific conditioning or training.

unconditional stimulus (UCS)   A stimulus that elicits a reflex without specific conditioning or training.

vesicle   Microscopic pouch or sac (about 40 billionths of a meter in diameter) that releases neurotransmitters from the axon terminal into the synaptic gap.

vicarious conditioning   Learning that occurs as a result of observing the behavior of others and the consequences their behavior produces.

voluntarism   A term describing the psychology of Wilhelm Wundt, who believed the mind is a volitional (choice-making) force.

voluntary behavior   Behavior in which an individual engages through a conscious decision to do so. The somatic nervous system controls many behaviors that psychologists would consider voluntary.

Wernicke's area   A small area of the left temporal lobe that plays a role in controlling language recognition.

BIBLIOGRAPHY

Allan, M. *Darwin and His Flowers.* London: Faber and Faber, 1977.

Ayllon, T., and N.H. Azrin. *The Token Economy: A Motivational System for Therapy and Rehabilitation.* New York: Appleton-Century-Crofts, 1968.

Bartlett, F.C. *Remembering: A Study in Experimental and Social Psychology.* Cambridge, UK: Cambridge University Press, 1932.

Beck, H. P., S. Levinson, and G. Irons (2009). Finding little Albert: A journey to John B. Watson's infant laboratory. *American Psychologist, 64,* 605–614.

Benjamin, L.T., Jr. *A Brief History of Modern Psychology.* Malden, Mass.: Blackwell Publishing, 2007.

———. *A History of Psychology in Letters*, 2nd ed. Malden, Mass.: Blackwell Publishing, 2006.

Bernstein, D.A., L.A. Penner, A. Clarke-Stewart, and E.J. Roy. *Psychology*, 8th ed. Boston: Houghton Mifflin Co., 2008.

Berry, J.W., Y.H. Poortinga, M.H. Segall, and P.R. Dasen. *Cross-Cultural Psychology: Research and Applications*, 2nd ed. Cambridge, UK: Cambridge University Press, 2002.

Best, J.B. *Cognitive Psychology*, 5th ed. Belmont, Calif.: Brooks/Cole, 1999.

Bjork, D.W. *B.F. Skinner: A Life.* New York: Basic Books, 1993.

Breedlove, S.M., M.R. Rosenzweig, and N.V. Watson. *Biological Psychology: An Introduction to Behavioral, Cognitive, and Clinical Neuroscience*, 5th ed. Sunderland, Mass.: Sinauer Associates, 2007.

Bronowski, J. *The Ascent of Man.* Boston: Little, Brown and Company, 1973.

Carlson, N.R. *Physiology of Behavior*, 6th ed. Boston: Allyn and Bacon, 1998.

Darwin, C. *On the Origin of Species by Means of Natural Selection, or the Preservation of Favoured Races in the Struggle for Life*. Cambridge, Mass: Harvard University Press, 1964 (Original work published 1859).

Davison, G.C., J.M. Neale, and A.M. Kring. *Abnormal Psychology*, 9th ed. New York: John Wiley & Sons, 2004.

Donnelly, M.E. (Ed.). *Reinterpreting the Legacy of William James*. Washington, D.C.: American Psychological Association, 1992.

Durant, W. *The Life of Greece*. New York: Simon and Schuster, 1939.

———. *The Renaissance: A History of Civilization in Italy from 1304-1576 A.D.* New York: Simon and Schuster, 1953.

Ebbinghaus, H. *Psychology: An Elementary Text-Book*. New York: Arno Press, 1973 [originally published in 1908].

Fancher, R.E. *Pioneers of Psychology: Studies of the Great Figures Who Paved the Way for the Contemporary Science of Behavior*. New York: W.W. Norton & Company, 1979.

Fernández-Armesto, F. *Millennium: A History of the Last Thousand Years*. New York: Scribner, 1995.

Flanagan, O.J., Jr. *The Science of the Mind*. Cambridge, Mass.: The MIT Press, 1984.

Flavell, J.H. *The Developmental Psychology of Jean Piaget*. New York: Van Nostrand, 1963.

Frankl, V. *Man's Search for Meaning*. New York: Washington Square, 1963.

Franklin, B. Operant reinforcement of prayer. *Journal of Applied Behavior Analysis* Vol. 2 (1969): 247.

Freud, S. *The Interpretation of Dreams*. In A.A. Brill (Ed.), *The Basic Writings of Sigmund Freud* (pp. 179-549). New York: Random House, 1938 (original work published 1900).

———. *An Outline of Psychoanalysis*. New York: W.W. Norton (Trans. J. Strachey; original work published 1940).

———. *The Standard Edition of the Complete Psychological Works of Sigmund Freud*, 24 vols. (J. Strachey, Ed.), 1953–1974. London: Hogarth Press.

Freud, S., and J. Breuer. *Studies on Hysteria*. Leipzeig: F. Deuticke, 1895.

Galotti, K.M. *Cognitive Psychology In and Out of the Laboratory*, 2nd ed. Belmont, Calif.: Brooks/Cole, 1999.

Galton, F. *Hereditary Genius*. London: Macmillan, 1869.

Gay, P. *Freud: A Life for Our Time*. New York: W.W. Norton, 1988.

Goodwin, C.J. *A History of Modern Psychology*, 3rd ed. New York: John Wiley & Sons, 2008.

Gould, S.J. *The Mismeasure of Man*. New York: W.W. Norton, 1981.

Greenwood, J.D. *A Conceptual History of Psychology*. New York: McGraw-Hill, 2009.

Guthrie, R.V. *Even the Rat Was White: A Historical View of Psychology*, 2nd ed. Boston: Allyn and Bacon, 1998.

Halpern, D.F. (Ed.). *Undergraduate Education in Psychology: A Blueprint for the Future of the Discipline*. Washington, D.C.: American Psychological Association, 2010.

Harris, B. (2011). Letting go of little Albert: Disciplinary memory, history, and the uses of myth. *Journal of the History of the Behavorial Sciences, 47*, 1–17.

Havemann, J. *A Life Shaken: My Encounter With Parkinson's Disease*. Baltimore: The Johns Hopkins University Press, 2002.

Heidbreder, E. *Seven Psychologies*. New York: Appleton-Century, 1933.

Hock, R.R. *Forty Studies That Changed Psychology: Explorations Into the History of Psychological Research*, 4th ed. Upper Saddle River, N.J.: Prentice-Hall, 2002.

Hofstede, G., and G.J. Hofstede. *Cultures and Organizations: Software of the Mind*, 2nd ed. New York: McGraw-Hill, 2005.

Hothersall, D. *History of Psychology*, 4th ed. Boston: McGraw-Hill, 2004.

Hunt, M. *The Story of Psychology*. New York: Anchor Books, 1994.

James, W. *The Principles of Psychology*. New York: Dover, 1890.

———. *Psychology: The Briefer Course*. New York: Harper & Row, 1961 (original work published 1892).

Joyce, N., and D.B. Baker. The Galton Whistle. *APS Observer* Vol. 22.(March 2009).

Kalat, J.W. *Biological Psychology*, 6th ed. Pacific Grove, Calif.: Brooks/Cole Publishing Co., 1998.

Keith, K.D. (Ed.). *Cross-Cultural Psychology: Contemporary Themes and Perspectives*. Malden, Mass.: Wiley-Blackwell, 2011.

Keller, F.S. *Summers and Sabbaticals: Selected Papers on Psychology and Education*. Champaign, Ill.: Research Press, 1977.

Kuhn, T.S. *The Structure of Scientific Revolutions*. Chicago: University of Chicago Press, 1962.

Makari, G. *Revolution in Mind: The Creation of Psychoanalysis*. New York: Harper, 2008.

Markus, H., and S. Kitayama. Culture and the Self: Implications for Cognition, Emotion, and Motivation. *Psychological Review* Vol. 98 (1991): 224–253.

Marx, M.H., and W.A. Hillix. *Systems and Theories in Psychology.* New York: McGraw-Hill, 1963.

Maslow, A. *Motivation and Personality.* New York: Harper, 1954.

Matsumoto, D. (Ed.). *The Cambridge Dictionary of Psychology.* Cambridge, UK: Cambridge University Press, 2009.

Matsumoto, D., and L. Juang. *Culture and Psychology*, 4th ed. Belmont, Calif.: Thomson-Wadsworth, 2008.

Miller, G.A. The Magical Number Seven, Plus or Minus Two: Some Limits on our Capacity for Processing Information. *Psychological Review* 63 (1956):81–97.

Mower, O.H., and W.A. Mowrer. Enuresis: A Method for Its Study and Treatment. *American Journal of Orthopsychiatry* Vol. 8 (1928): 436–447.

Myers, D.G. *Psychology*, 9th ed. New York: Worth Publishers, 2010.

Patoine, B. Brain-Machine Interfaces: Sci-fi Concepts Make Clinical Inroads. In B. Mauk (Ed.), *2009 Progress Report on Brain Research.* New York: The Dana Alliance for Brain Initiatives, 2009. p. 43–52.

Pervin, L.A., D. Cervone, and O.P. John. *Personality: Theory and Research*, 9th ed. New York: Wiley, 2005.

Pickren, W.E., and A. Rutherford. *A History of Modern Psychology in Context.* Hoboken, N.J.: John Wiley & Sons, 2010.

Proctor, R.W., and E.J. Capaldi. *Why Science Matters: Understanding the Methods of Psychological Research.* Malden, Mass.: Blackwell, 2006.

Raymo, C. *Skeptics and True Believers: The Exhilarating Connection Between Science and Religion.* New York: Walker and Company, 1998.

Roberts, J.M. *History of the World.* New York: Oxford University Press, 1993.

Rogers, C.R. *On Becoming a Person.* Boston: Houghton-Mifflin, 1961.

Rose, S.P.R. *Future Directions in Neuroscience: A Twenty Year Timescale.* Presented at Unfolding the Mind: Prospects and Perils in Neuroscience. Auckland, NZ, March, 2007. Available at: www.morst.govt.nz/current-work/futurewatch/neuroscience/stephen-rose.

Rutherford, A. *Beyond the Box: B.F. Skinner's Technology of Behavior from Laboratory to Life, 1950s-1970s.* Toronto: University of Toronto Press, 2009.

Schultz, D. *A History of Modern Psychology*, 3rd ed. New York: Academic Press, 1981.

Scoville, W.B., and B. Milner. Loss of recent memory after bilateral hippocampal lesions. *The Journal of Neurology, Neurosurgery, and Psychiatry* Vol. 20 (1957):11–21.

Seligman, M.E.P. *Learned Optimism: How to Change Your Mind and Your Life*. New York: Simon & Schuster, 1998.

Skinner, B.F. *About Behaviorism*. New York: Knopf, 1974.

———. *A Matter of Consequences*. New York: Knopf, 1984.

———. *Particulars of My Life*. New York: Knopf, 1976.

———. *Science and Human Behavior*. New York: Macmillan, 1953.

———. *The Shaping of a Behaviorist*. New York: Knopf, 1979.

———. *Walden Two*. New York: Macmillan, 1948.

Skinner, B.F., & C. Ferster. *Schedules of Reinforcement*. New York: Appleton-Century-Crofts, 1957.

Sternberg, R.J. *Psychology: In Search of the Human Mind*, 3rd ed. Fort Worth: Harcourt, 2001.

Tarpy, R.M. *Contemporary Learning Theory and Research*. New York: McGraw-Hill, 1997.

Tavris, C., and E. Aronson. *Mistakes Were Made (But Not by Me)*. Orlando, Fl: Harcourt, 2007

Terman, L.M. *The Measurement of Intelligence*. Boston: Houghton Mifflin, 1916.

Thorndike, E.L. *Animal Intelligence*. New York: Macmillan, 1911.

Watson, J.B. *Behaviorism*. Chicago: The University of Chicago Press, 1961 (original work published 1924).

———. *Psychological Care of Infant and Child*. New York: Norton, 1928.

———. Psychology as the behaviorist views it. *Psychological Bulletin* Vol. 6 (1913):57–58.

Wittrock, M.C. (Ed.). *The Human Brain*. Englewood Cliffs, N.J.: Prentice-Hall, Inc.

Woodworth, R.S. *Contemporary Schools of Psychology*. New York: Ronald, 1948.

Wundt, W. *Principles of Physiological Psychology*, 5th ed. New York: Macmillan, 1904. (Trans. E.B. Titchener, original work published 1874).

Yalom, I.D. *Existential Psychotherapy*. New York: Basic Books, 1980.

INDEX

Index note: Page numbers followed by *g* indicate glossary entries.